ZAINAB FASIKI

HSHOUMA

SHAME! BODIES AND SEXUALITY IN MOROCCO

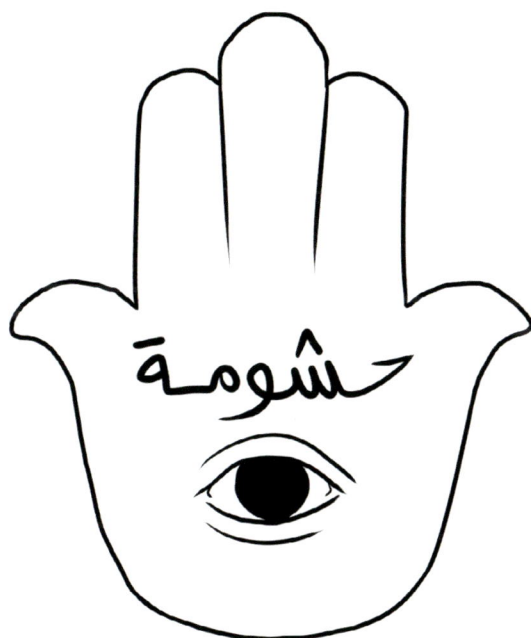

حشومة

CLAIRVIEW

In my country, our bodies and sexual relationships are standardized by state laws, but also by Islam, Moroccan culture, family traditions and society. The multiplicity of these norms (political, religious and socio-cultural) generates frustration in the population – a sexual and emotional lack – which translates into sexual violence such as harassment and rape. In Morocco, some people claim: 'Hshouma is necessary for a healthy society', but unfortunately this word hshouma (or lheshma) is actually the source of many problems, and this is what I'm going to demonstrate in this book.

حشومة

حشومة

North Africa was once inhabited by the Amazighs, renowned for their great respect for women. In the 7th century, the Arabs took control of this region and completely transformed it. To do so, they won the battle against Dihya Tadmut (also known as Kahina). This Amazigh warrior-queen had united the Maghreb (North Africa), doing her best to protect her country until her death in 703. With the Muslim conquest came the beginning of male domination.

Many have described Kahina as one of the first feminists in history. Unfortunately, as a result of various historical upheavals, North African women subsequently lost their prestige and freedom. Today, the Amazigh community is still fighting to speak out about its culture, but also about the ever-worsening condition of women

In addition to the Amazighs, many Moroccans feel a gap between their convictions and the norms imposed in their country. But it's still *hshouma* – or shameful – as well as illegal, to express one's thoughts freely. This culture of shame has oppressed innocent souls, destroyed hundreds of thousands of lives, frustrated powerful desires and led to numerous crimes.

A majority of Moroccans believe that hiding bodies, limiting sexuality and freedoms gives value to society and maintains order. But the fact that they refuse to tolerate those who do not share their vision confirms that terrorism has many faces... Coexistence between us must be discussed so that there is no more *hshouma* relating to this subject. We are living through a social and sexual crisis and it must be resolved.

Added to this are media propaganda, fundamentalism and Islamism, which encourage the faithful to impose their beliefs on others, and even to attack those who do not submit to Moroccan social norms.

I didn't write this book in the Moroccan language, because we don't even have the right words in *Darija* (the dialect spoken in Morocco) to talk about sexuality. Over time, our words have taken on a negative connotation, and we use them as insults. For example, there is no term in *Darija* to describe genitalia with objectivity, or sexuality with respect.

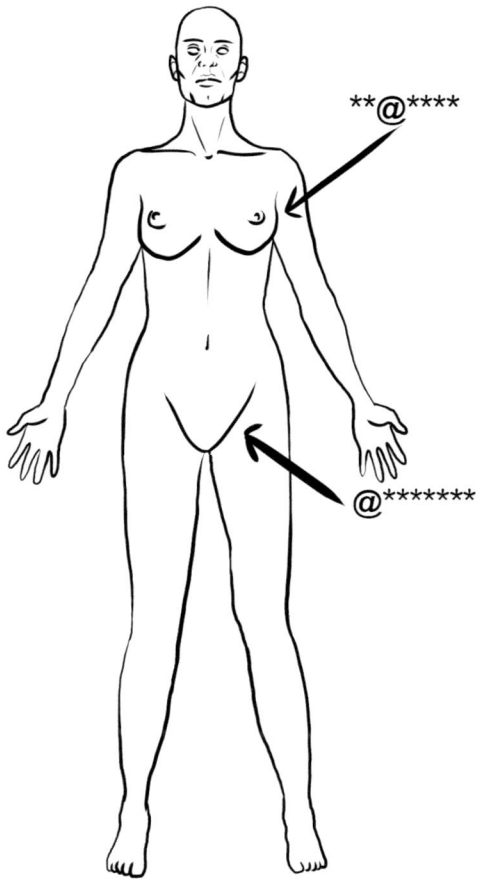

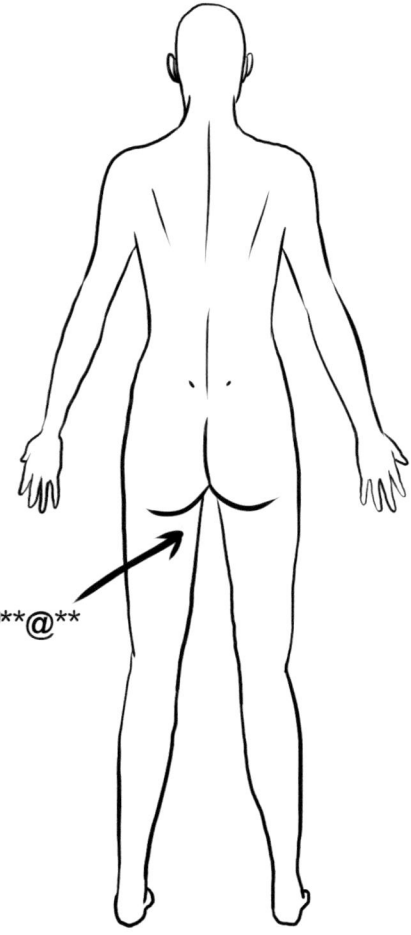

@**

@*******

@

This vocabulary exists in Arabic, Amazigh and French (considered one of the main languages since colonization), but most Moroccan families don't speak these languages. *Darija* is the most common language in Morocco, so if it doesn't have the words to name taboos, how are we going to break them?

I DON'T FIGHT THE IDEAS OF MY
COUNTRY FOR FUN... IF YOU THINK
I'M EXAGGERATING, I'D LIKE YOU TO
BE A WOMAN IN MOROCCO FOR A DAY.
THEN YOU CAN INFORM ME HOW THIS
EXPERIENCE WAS FOR YOU.

IF I TAKE UP THE PEN, IT'S NOT FOR
THE PLEASURE OF CRITICIZING MY
SOCIETY, BUT BECAUSE I WANT IT TO
BE BETTER, TO BE BASED ON PEACE,
ALLOWING EVERYONE TO LIVE AS THEY
PLEASE, AND OF COURSE, BECAUSE I
LOVE MOROCCO AND MOROCCANS.

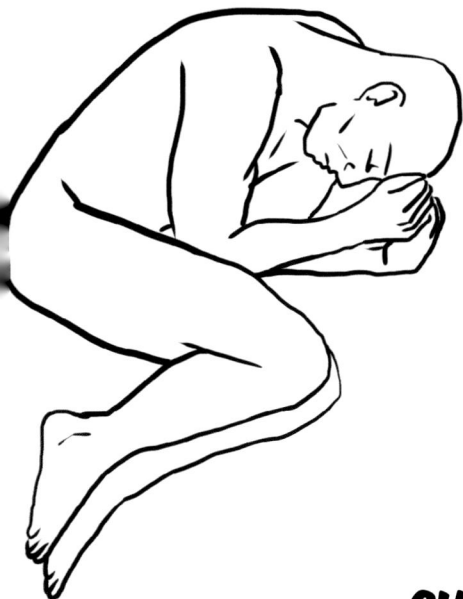

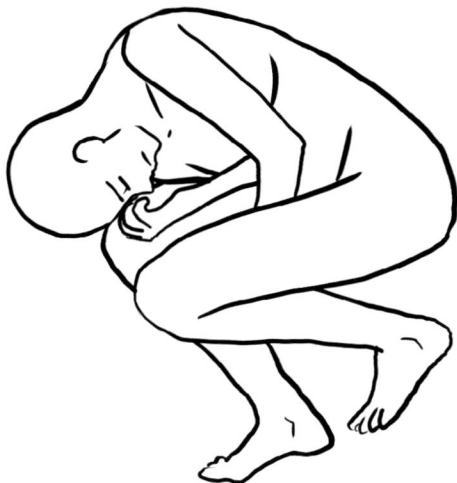

CHAPTER 1

THE BODY

The body is our material envelope, a set of
intelligent mechanisms, but unfortunately
a certain number of Moroccans only see
its sexual dimension. As a result,
the body is valued if it is hidden,
and punished if it is exposed.

1. LIBERATING NUDITY

Nudity is uniquely associated with sexuality. It is synonymous with shame, impurity and sacrilege. This leads to this reality: the more the body is hidden, the more it is respected. Being naked diminishes the value of individuals and the respect due to them, especially when it comes to Moroccan women. Exposed to the judgments of others, they don't dress the way they want to. Nudity, whether partial or total, is not accepted; on the contrary, it is punished. However, I believe that hiding women's bodies and seeing them only as sexual objects only leads to increased frustration and violence (harassment, rape, etc.).

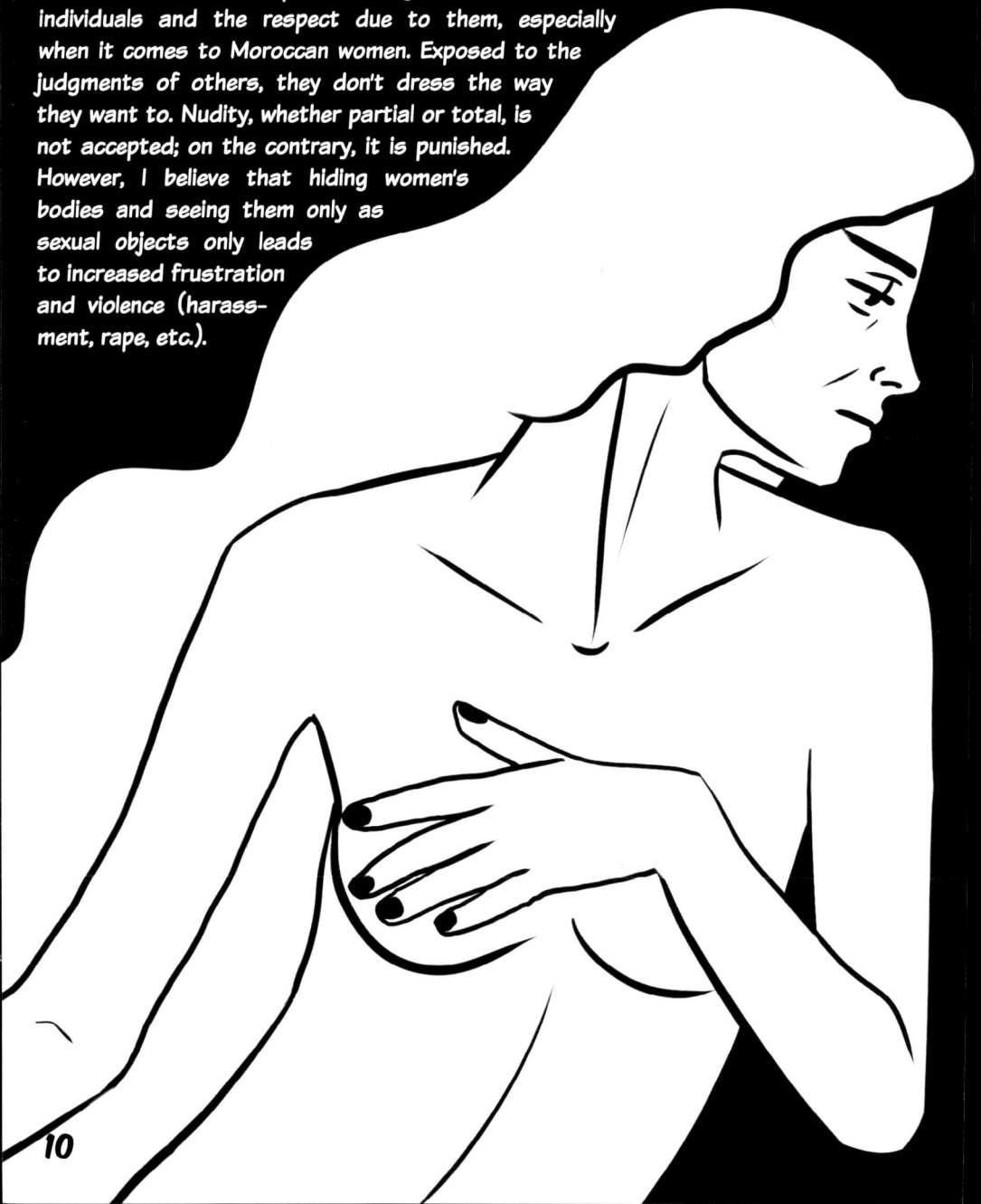

What if we looked at bodies in a
non-sexual way?

What if we tolerated nudity in art and
stopped censorship?

Would bodies in public spaces still
bother other people?

But getting there isn't that simple, we have to face
up to many different viewpoints, and take things
one step at a time

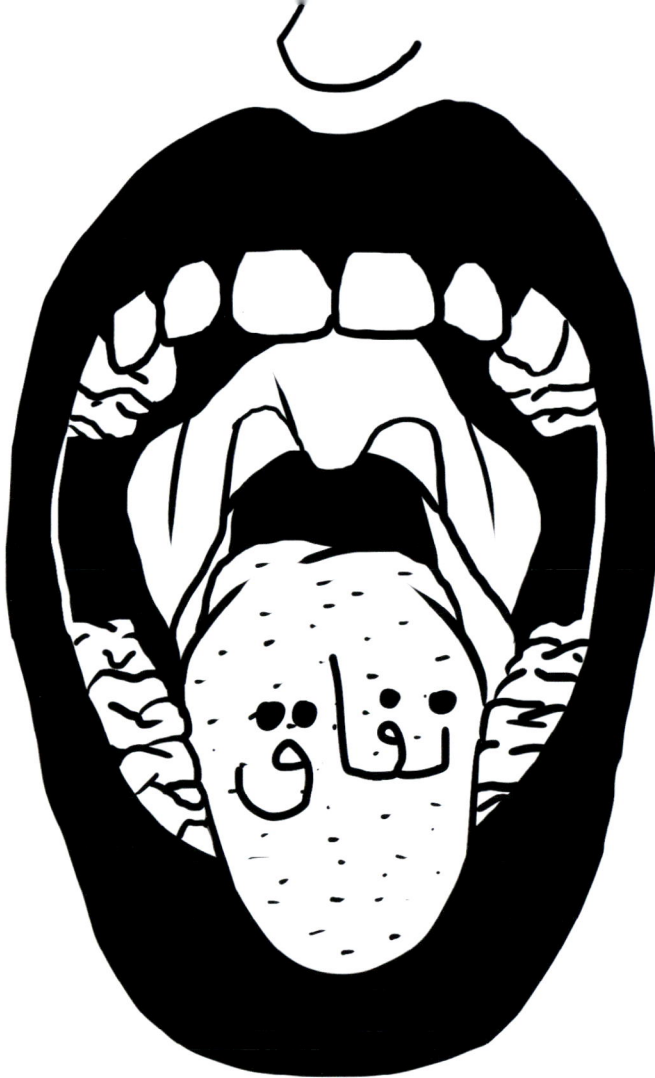

The majority of the Moroccan population is Muslim, and believes that religious laws are eternal. Some even consider nudity to be stupid, because we are civilized beings and therefore should rise above our bodies. Others say that 'liberating bodies' is a form of extremism. And then there are those who imagine that breaking the nudity taboo means inviting everyone to be naked in the street. No! We want to liberate the expression of nudity in art and society, which is different!

THIS BOOK IS NOT ABOUT
IMPOSING IDEAS OR CHANGING
BELIEFS. I'M WRITING IT IN ORDER
TO TALK ABOUT AN OPPRESSED
MOROCCAN COMMUNITY — OF
WHICH I'M A PART — BECAUSE OUR
LIFESTYLE CHOICES ARE HSHOUMA
FOR SOCIETY. I WRITE IN ORDER
TO INVITE ALL MOROCCANS TO
COEXIST WITH THEIR DIFFERENCES.
IF YOU'RE ONE OF THOSE WHO ARE
AGAINST NUDITY, YOU SHOULD
KNOW THAT TRUE PEACE LIES IN
ACCEPTING OTHERS AND THEIR
DIFFERENCES. NOT EVERYONE HAS
TO BE LIKE YOU!

As a result, nudity has a bad reputation. It's frowned upon by conservatives, intellectuals, even feminists, not to mention the hypocrites who, being fans of pornography, bizarrely condemn nudity in art (we're living a social schizophrenia). It's always linked to stupidity and sex. My dear readers, intelligence doesn't mean avoiding nudity because it's a symbol of desire, but rather making a distinction. Of course, the body gives rise to desire and excitement, but if this is the case every time we see a body in art or everyday life, then there's a problem! And besides, if women have to hide their bodies so that men don't get aroused, why don't men hide theirs too? Because we also have desires!

14

I'VE OFTEN BEEN TOLD THAT
DEFENDING NUDITY ISN'T BEING
FEMINIST, AND THAT WOMEN
WILL BE STRONG WHEN THEY
BECOME GREAT PERSONALITIES
OR RENOWNED SCIENTISTS. BUT,
WHATEVER HER PROFESSION, IF
A WOMAN WANTS TO WEAR A
TWO-PIECE SWIMSUIT OR SLEEP
WITH WHOMEVER SHE CHOOSES,
I CAN ASSURE YOU THAT SHE'LL
BE INSULTED BY EVERYONE,
ESPECIALLY IF SHE'S MOROCCAN!

Women's bodies are always viewed through the eyes of men.
For example, when a woman is naked, she's insulted
because it excites men, and when she's covered up,
she's insulted for the simple reason that she has to
remain attractive to her husband.
But our lives don't revolve around men.
A woman can cover or undress because
she wants to for herself.

2. BODY TRANSFORMATIONS

Our bodies function, in a way, mechanically...
For reproduction to be possible, sexual intercourse must take place during the period of ovulation, with penetration of the penis into the vagina. An egg is expelled from the ovary around 14 days after the first day of the last menstrual period, depending on the length of the cycle. For pregnancy to occur, the egg must be fertilized by a sperm. The fusion of these two elements results in a single cell, which gives rise to the embryo. It then continues its journey to the uterus.

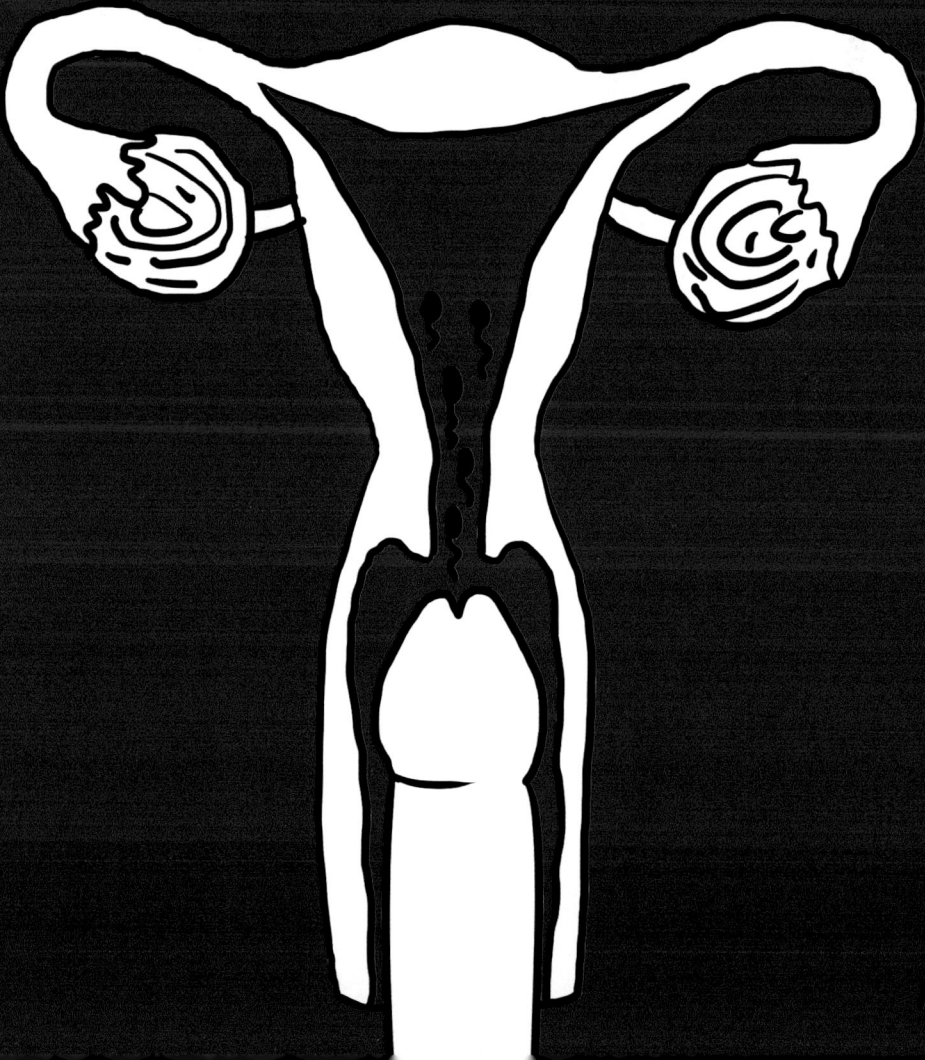

After the cell division of this egg, the organs that make up a human being are gradually formed. When the fertilized egg attaches to the mucous membrane, implantation occurs. At this stage, the egg has two layers: an inner part and an outer part which transforms into a placenta to protect the embryo, nourish it and form its nervous system.

The embryo develops over several weeks. From the ninth, the genitalia begin to appear. By the eleventh week, the embryo has become a foetus, with all the vital systems and organs almost fully developed. After nine months of pregnancy, childbirth takes place.

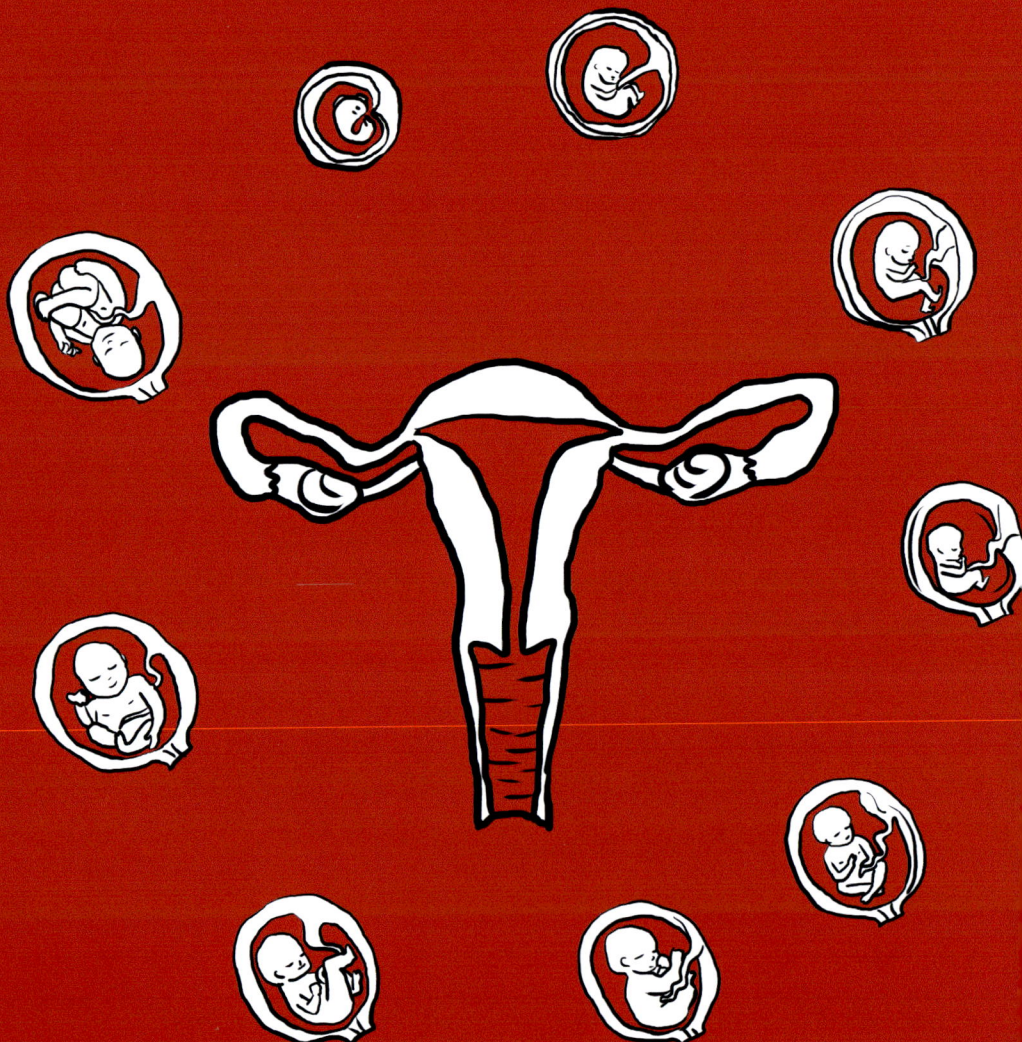

From birth, our bodies are labelled:
feminine or masculine, pink or blue.

Explaining the body using the words 'girl' and 'boy' makes me
uncomfortable... Gender identity is still a big taboo!
The word 'man' is assigned to people with a penis,
and 'women' to people with a vagina.
But there are some individuals who have both.

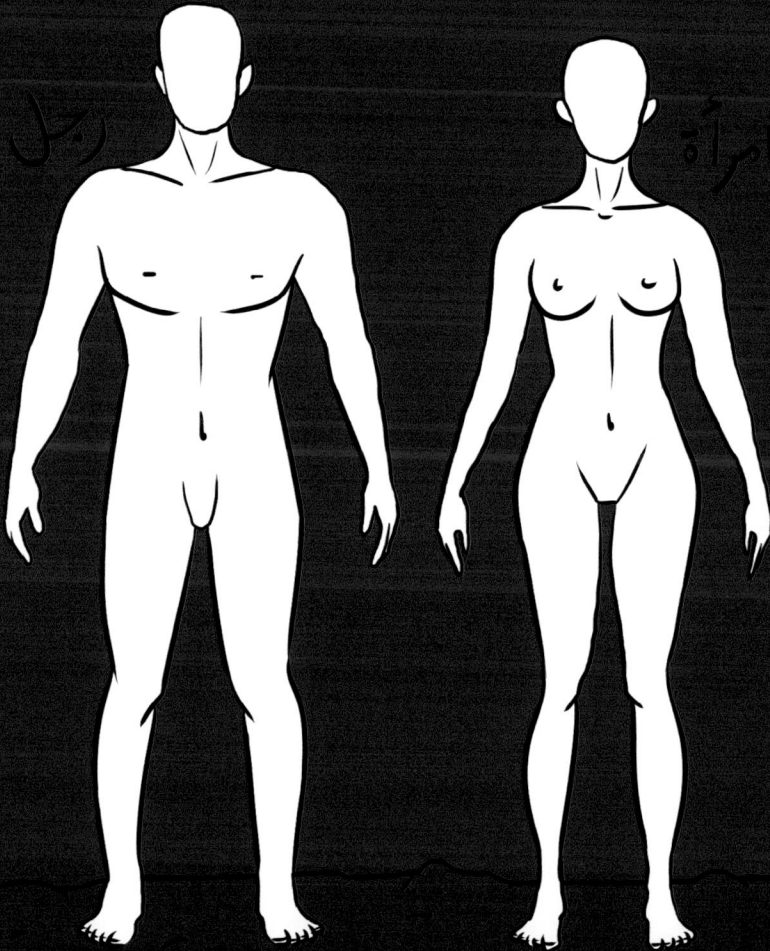

رجل

امرأة

I've met several people (including Moroccans) who feel they're
living with an imposed gender that doesn't suit them,
and unfortunately, for having decided to change it,
they are threatened with death. It is to fight against this gender
prejudice that I prefer to explain puberty with the terms XX and XY.
In my opinion, they are the most neutral, in terms of social or
linguistic norms. In my view, after puberty, the individual is able to
choose their identity: female, male or other. That's how I see it.

For most mammals, including us, sexual differentiation is genetically determined by the XY system. Each cell in the human body contains 23 pairs of chromosomes in its nucleus: 22 pairs are autosomes, and the 23rd is a sex chromosome pair containing the XY system. When the system contains two X (XX) chromosomes, the individual will have a uterus, breasts, a clitoris, and so on. When it has one X chromosome and one Y chromosome (XY), the individual will have testicles, a penis, and so on. The egg always represents the X, but the sperm can be either an X or a Y. So an X egg fertilized by a Y sperm gives an XY foetus, and an X egg fertilized by an X sperm gives an XX foetus.

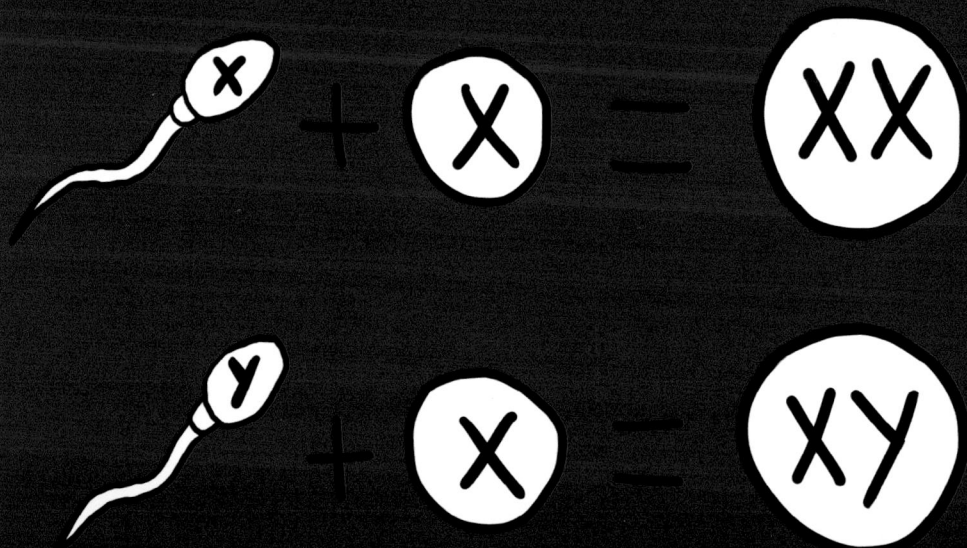

$$X + X = XX$$

$$Y + X = XY$$

The Y chromosome is the element that defines our genitalia, carrying the SRY (sex-determining region of Y chromosome) gene. The presence of this gene leads to a genital system with testicles, penis, etc. The absence of this gene leads to a genital system containing uterus, clitoris, etc. In the case of intersex individuals, this gene may be on the X chromosome but not on the Y, so a mutation of this gene results in XY individuals but with sexual characteristics similar to those of XX. As scientific studies have shown, if an XX individual receives this gene, he or she will have sexual characteristics similar to those of XY. The presence of the SRY gene defines the nature of sexual characteristics in an XX or an XY.

So, during embryonic development, the 23rd chromosome pair determines our reproductive system, in particular the primary sexual characteristics of the gonads (ovaries and testes) and genitalia (internal and external), but also the secondary sexual characteristics that define sexual behaviour, and the physical traits that distinguish XX from XY. The gonads are the reproductive organs: the ovaries in XX, the testes in XY. These organs produce the reproductive cells known as gametes: spermatozoa from the testicles, oocytes (developing eggs) from the ovaries.

BUT WE'VE ALWAYS ASSOCIATED
XX WITH WOMEN AND XY WITH MEN,
WHEREAS WE SOMETIMES MEET
XY INDIVIDUALS WHO FEEL LIKE WOMEN.
WE'LL SAY 'THIS MAN LIVES LIKE A WOMAN'
OR 'HE'S EFFEMINATE', WHEREAS IN REALITY
HE IDENTIFIES AS A WOMAN. TO BE FAIR,
WE'D HAVE TO SAY 'SHE'S A WOMAN'!
PEOPLE WITH PENISES WHO LIVE AS WOMEN
ARE INSULTED AND SOMETIMES EVEN
KILLED IN MOROCCAN SOCIETY.
IF INDIVIDUALS WITH A PENIS AND
FEMININITY EXIST, WHY DO WE CONTINUE
TO ASSOCIATE FEMININITY ONLY WITH
INDIVIDUALS WITH A VAGINA?

And sex hormones play a major role.
Oestrogens and progesterone are secreted
by the ovaries in XX people, and androgens, including
testosterone, are produced by the testes in XY people.
But in fact, both XX and XY people can have all these
hormones at the same time, and their proportions
vary from one individual to another.

CONCLUSION:

THE PHRASE 'I'M A WOMAN IN A MAN'S BODY' IS FALSE, BECAUSE THERE'S NO SUCH THING AS A MAN'S OR WOMAN'S BODY. AND THIS PERCEPTION CAN CHANGE OVER THE YEARS. A PERSON IS FREE TO EXPRESS HIS OR HER GENDER AS WOMAN, MAN, ANDROGYNOUS, AGENDER, BIGENDER, TRIGENDER, CISGENDER, INTERSEX, NON-BINARY, GENDERQUEER, TWO-SPIRIT, TRANS, AND SO ON. THOSE EXPERIENCING GENDER DYSPHORIA CAN, FINALLY, LIVE WITH THE ONE THAT SUITS THEM, AS IS THE CASE WITH TRANSGENDER PEOPLE, FOR EXAMPLE. THE TRANSITION PROCESS CAN INCLUDE HORMONE THERAPY, SURGERY...

I know, all these words still enclose our choices in labels, but I think it's a necessary language, in my society, to start understanding differences. And once these problems of understanding are solved, we'll be able to free ourselves from labels once and for all. This will be a big step forward, allowing others to live as they wish. In some countries, you even have to ask the person whether you should use 'he' or 'she' or another pronoun.

THE TRANSITION FROM CHILDHOOD TO ADULTHOOD IS CALLED PUBERTY. DURING ADOLESCENCE, CHANGES TAKE PLACE AS MESSAGES FROM THE BRAIN STIMULATE THE ENDOCRINE GLANDS (OVARIES AND TESTES) TO PRODUCE SEX HORMONES. BY THE END OF PUBERTY, THE SEXUAL ORGANS AND THE BODY ARE DEVELOPED, AND THE INDIVIDUAL IS FINALLY ABLE TO REPRODUCE.

For the XX age group (between 10 and 14), the ovaries begin to produce hormones such as oestrogen, the breasts swell, hair begins to grow in the sexual areas and under the armpits, the lips of the vulva enlarge, the pelvis widens, the body becomes rounder in the hips, stomach and buttocks, white discharge and menstruation appear.

For XYs (aged 11 to 15), testicles enlarge and testosterone production increases, the penis grows, the scrotum becomes pigmented, the voice changes, and facial, chest and sexual hair appears.

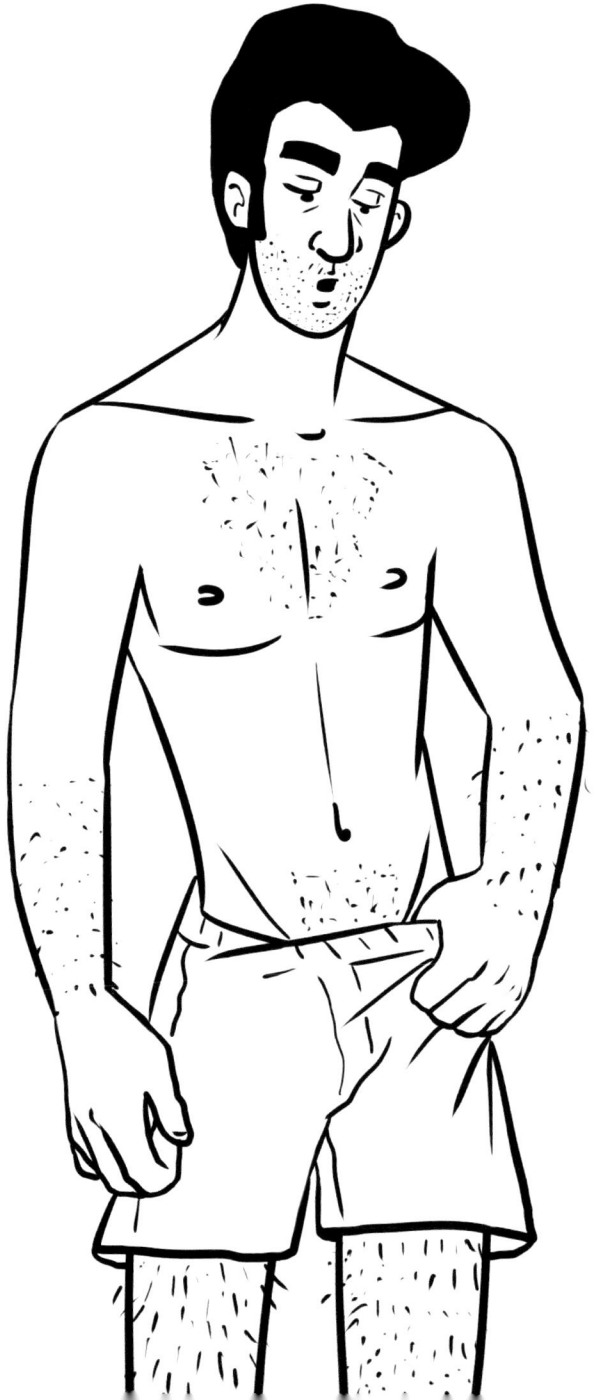

FOR XX AND XY, ACNE IS CAUSED BY HORMONES, WHICH ARE ALSO RESPONSIBLE FOR SEXUAL DESIRE AND EROTIC DREAMS — AND OF COURSE, HORMONES ARE ALSO INVOLVED IN PSYCHOLOGICAL CHANGES SUCH AS ANXIETY

Our bodies blossom as we enter
puberty and adulthood, but they
also undergo the process of aging,
when skin, hair and all organs begin
to weaken. After death, our bodies
decompose, leaving only our bones...

I speak of the life cycle of our
bodies in order to invite you to think
differently, to reflect on how our
bodies are works of art. Whatever
our beliefs... censoring our bodies,
or reducing them to sex, is a crime
against the extraordinary years in
which they develop!

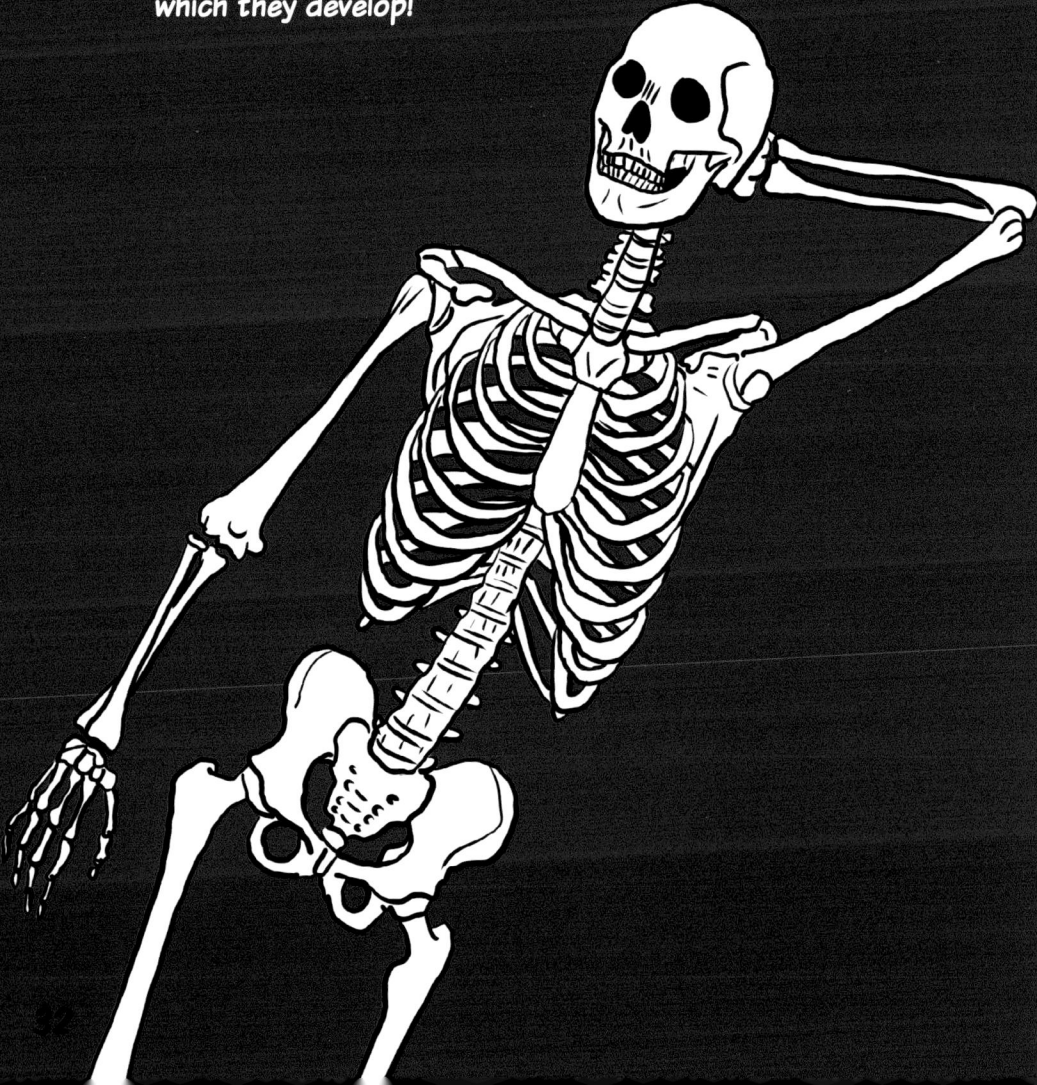

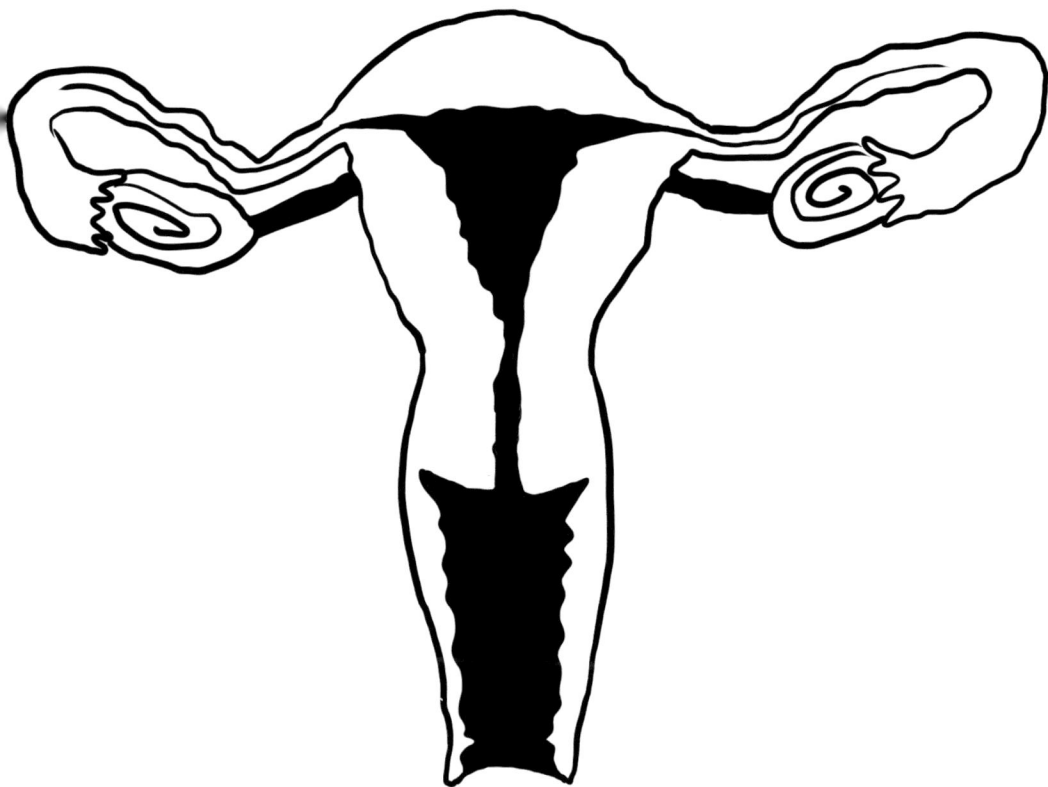

Here we come to the most *hshouma* part...
the anatomy of the genitalia!

The XX genital system consists of two glands (the ovaries)
that produce eggs, and two fallopian tubes that carry these eggs
to the uterus, where they can be fertilized. The organs of copulation
are the vulva – the set of external genitalia comprising labia minora,
labia majora, vulval vestibule, vaginal orifice and urethra – and the
clitoris, which surrounds the vagina and urethra, visible at the top of
the labia minora. The clitoris plays a major role in sexual desire and
orgasm. The vagina is an internal genital organ, the muscular tube that
opens at the vulva, is in contact with the uterus, and is penetrated
during sexual intercourse. The erogenous G-spot, located 2 to 5 cm
from the vaginal entrance, is a source of orgasm if stimulated.

It's also through the vagina that our menstrual fluid flows. In conservative Moroccan families, when you menstruate, you may be excluded from certain family, social, cultural, sporting and religious activities, because your body is considered impure. But that's not true!

Menstrual fluid is made up of blood, cells from the endometrial mucosa in the uterus and mucus. Our body eliminates these elements that support a pregnancy, if fertilization does not occur. Ovulation is almost monthly (the cycle varies from 25 to 32 days) and the average menstrual period lasts between three days and a week.

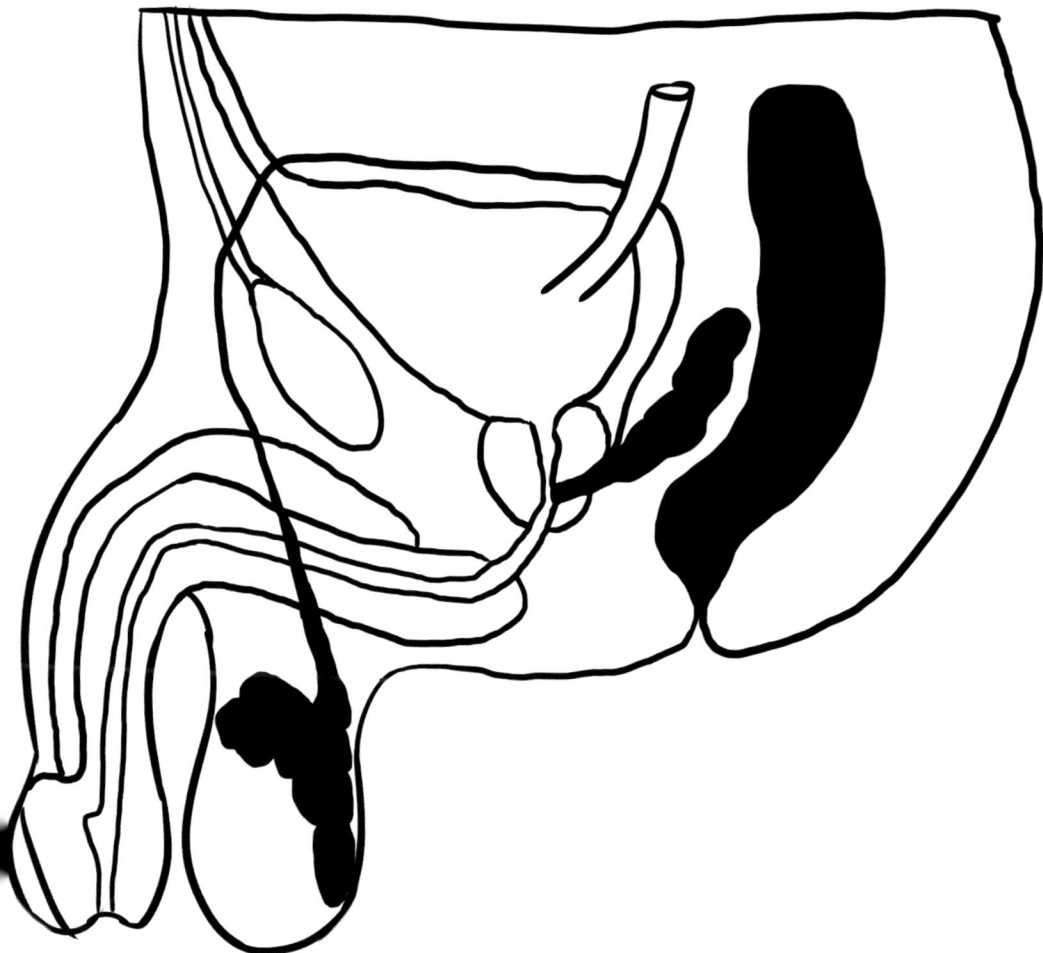

The XY genitalia consists of the penis, which contains the urethra for the passage of sperm and urine. The erection of the penis is caused by the relaxation of its muscles. Some people believe that penis size affects pleasure during intercourse, but this is not true. The G-spot is only a few centimetres from the entrance to the vagina, so a small penis doesn't reduce pleasure! And if it's big, you just have to relax the vagina. But beware, there's also the P-spot for XY men, which can be reached by stimulating the prostate gland, which still remains a huge taboo today! Then there are the testicles, where sperm and testosterone are produced. And, of course, the two glands inside the body, the prostate and the seminal vesicles, which help produce seminal fluid. The latter, once mixed with the spermatozoa, gives the semen that is expelled during ejaculation. The sensitive part of the penis is the glans at the tip, which is always covered by a skin called the prepuce (or foreskin), but during an erection, the glans is uncovered and the foreskin remains behind. Of course, the foreskin is the part of the penis that Muslims and Jews circumcise.

Don't hesitate to discover
your genitals, for they conceal
a whole world of pleasure,
and above all,
keep them healthy!

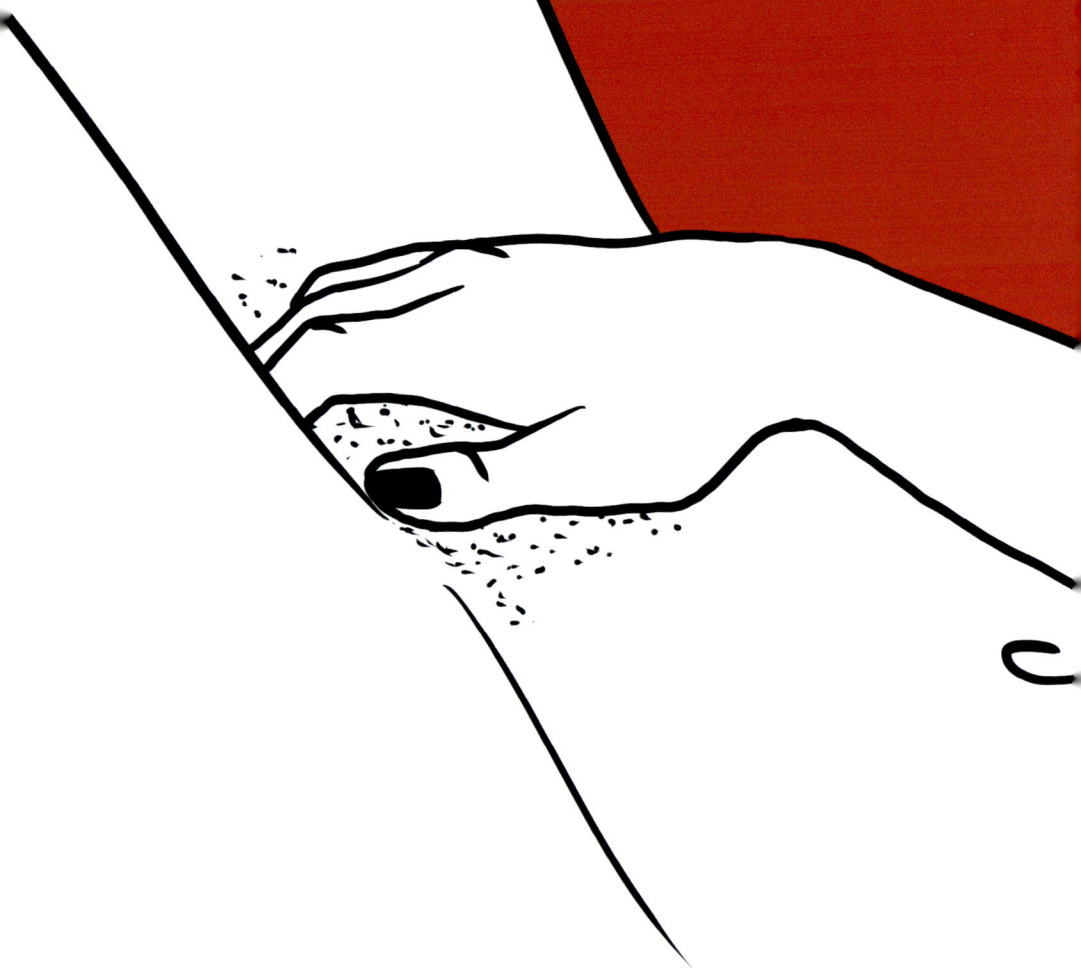

3. BODY DIVERSITY

The media disseminate a representation of our bodies that is out of step with reality (models, influencers on social media networks, advertising, magazines, films, beauty products, etc.), and since talking about our bodies is taboo, it's very difficult to deconstruct it. This leads people to compare their bodies to models, and to resort to plastic surgery at increasingly younger ages.

Using men's fantasies has always been the ideal marketing strategy for companies, sometimes even to sell products that have nothing to do with women. Unfortunately, it works well, as they continue to attract more and more customers and earn more and more money.

The media have imposed an image of the physically perfect woman that excludes those who do not correspond to this perception of beauty, whether because of their weight, age, figure, disability, skin colour, body hair...

مام الحرية

In Morocco and other African countries, there's a lot of propaganda promoting European and American beauty. I hope that women in these regions are discovering just how unique their beauty is! And I'm still dreaming that the media, magazines and beauty contests will start to show African splendour. The moral of this story is: let's not hesitate to fall in love with our bodies, every time we're in front of a mirror.

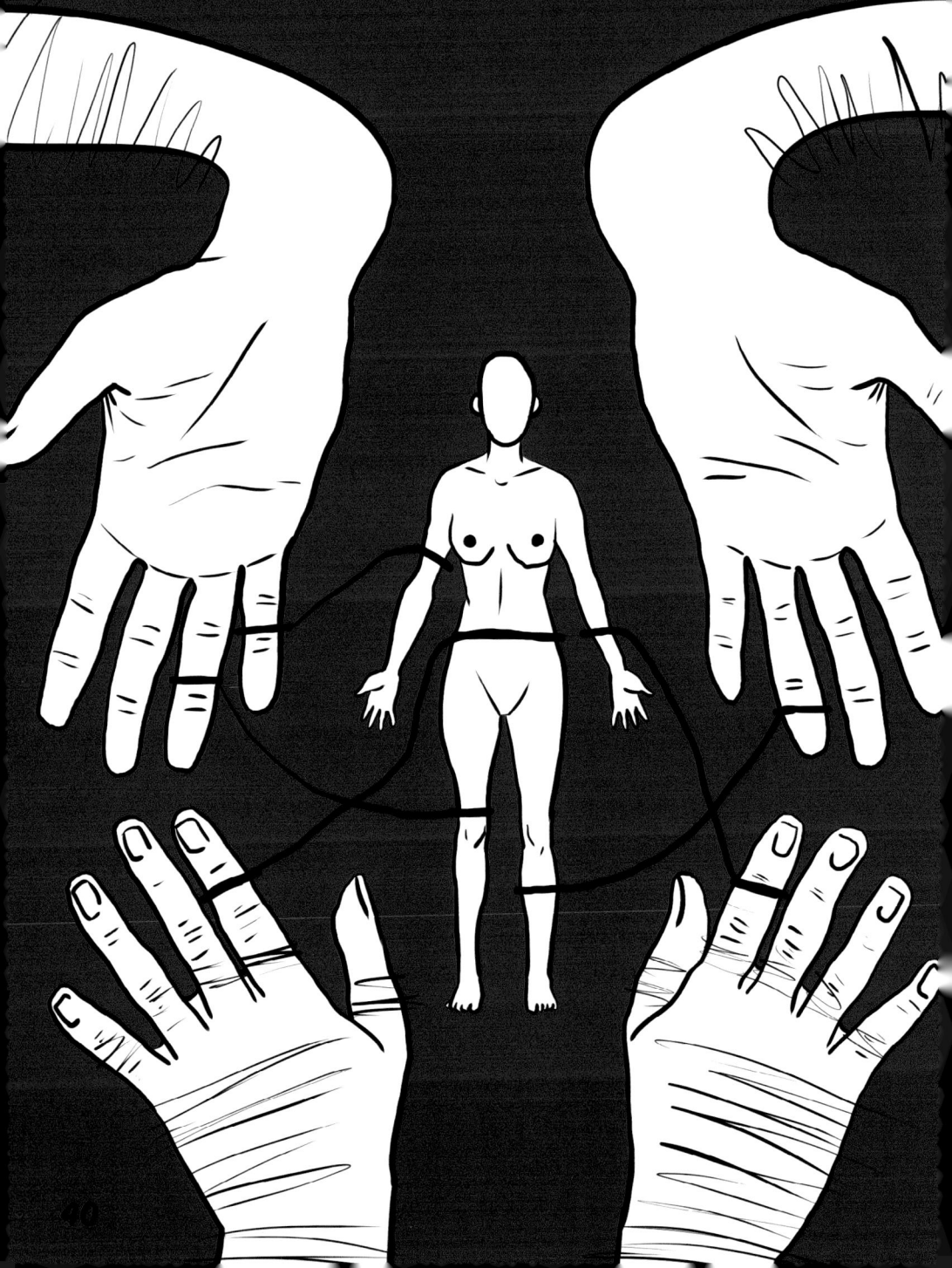

4. BODILY FREEDOM

Our bodies, especially women's, are subject to the scrutiny of others – parents, brothers and neighbours – who reserve for themselves the right to judge us.

Before going out, we must always ask if we are putting ourselves in danger. Danger varies according to when and where you go: home, beach, café, work, street, public transport, school, night, morning... To be safe, you need to own your own car (or have a dog, become a black belt in karate...) but this is not possible for most Moroccan women. With the development of a virtual society, the gaze of others is also present online, for example through the observations and judgements on social networks. Today, Moroccan women's bodies – in terms of their sexuality, style of dress and freedom of movement – belong to society.

أنا متعبة
جدا

For some parents, it is their child who will make the family's reputation. That's why they're disappointed to give birth to a girl, because they know they'll face many problems when she grows up.

A woman's body is literally the 'image' of the family, but this doesn't apply to men's bodies... because they're men! Patriarchy still reigns in Morocco, due to tradition, culture and religion. So, parents need to bring up their children as equals, and stop the propaganda that makes us believe that men's bodies are the best!

What's more, men maintain the patriarchal model because it's financially and politically advantageous to them, and it's now a question of power and money. Some even declare that it's God's will, simply in order to reinforce their ideology.

But religion is not the only culprit. Let's not forget how women's bodies are oppressed under the capitalist regime, exploited in factories all over the world, particularly in poorer regions. Some of these companies even manufacture products for feminists and are run by women – renowned for their strength and independence...

And let's not forget that most of us feel obliged to wear heels, make-up and 'make an effort' to be attractive... This is also the case for metrosexuals, those city-dwellers who often take care of their appearance under pressure from society.

So, hiding our bodies isn't the answer! On the contrary, we have to let them be. Yes, our breasts and nipples too... If I show them, I'm not inviting a sexual relationship, and if you think so... it's up to you to heal your uncontrolled desires. Let's stop always linking the body to sex – they're two separate things!

CHAPTER 2
SEXUALITY

The continuity of humanity is based on reproduction through sexual relations. Sexual relations have not always been regulated, but today they are codified by institutions and laws. The aim? To organize a peaceful life in order to avoid rape, control reproduction and defend the rights of individuals.

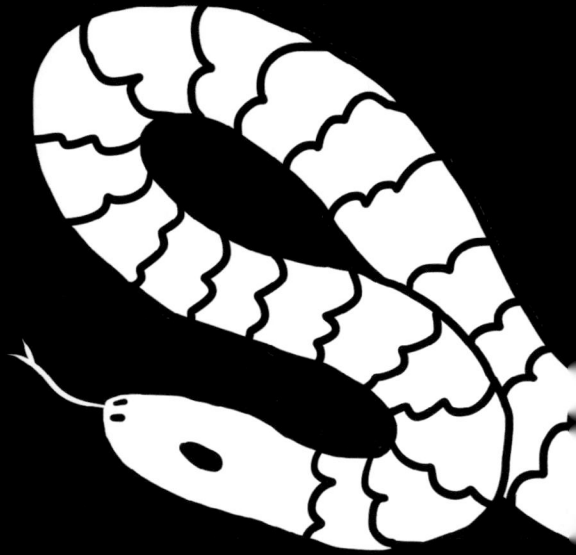

Unfortunately, in most countries, these codes limit
our sexual freedom. Instead of organizing our lives,
they create even more frustration and crime.
Sexuality is a natural human need, so if it is controlled,
it can only lead to chaos within our social system...

I'D LIKE TO REPEAT ONCE AGAIN...
I DON'T WANT TO CHANGE ANY RELIGION
OR BELIEF... MY PHILOSOPHY HAS ALWAYS
BEEN TO RESPECT ALL COMMUNITIES, AND
NEVER TO DESPISE OR MOCK ANY OF THEM.

BUT I'M COMMITTED TO HUMAN RIGHTS.
LIVING UNDER A REGIME THAT PENALIZES
SEXUAL RELATIONS OUTSIDE MARRIAGE,
OTHER SEXUAL ORIENTATIONS, MARRYING
NON-MUSLIMS, GIVING BIRTH OUTSIDE
MARRIAGE... ONLY MEANS THAT
FUNDAMENTAL RIGHTS ARE NOT
RESPECTED, ESPECIALLY FOR NON-MUSLIM
MOROCCANS WHO ARE OBLIGED TO FOLLOW
THESE STANDARDS. SEX WITH CONSENT,
WHATEVER THE SEXUAL ORIENTATION,
THE PLACE OR THE CONTEXT IN WHICH IT IS
PRACTICED, DOES NO HARM TO ANYONE.

Respecting all communities also means that Moroccan
Muslims can live by their own rules, and non-Muslims
by theirs. Let's not forget that Morocco brings
together citizens of different religions, beliefs
and ethnicities. Respecting the fundamental freedome
of each community will therefore be a prerequisite
for peace in my wonderful country.

سلام تعايش حب

But it won't be easy. The definition of family in my culture is: a marriage between a mother and a father + children. But this definition is not always valid! On the one hand, human beings evolve over time. And on the other, this model hasn't always existed. Homosexuality, for example, was once accepted in the MENA region (Middle East and North Africa). My point is simply that human beings are not all the same!

Separated or divorced Western families are still a nightmare
and a sin for the Middle East and North Africa. For us,
it means that a society is not healthy. But where is
the healthy society in Morocco today? Can we recognize
that, with our current laws, we are experiencing a social failure?

BELIEVE ME, IT'S A CURSE TO
LIVE IN A COUNTRY WHERE
NOBODY UNDERSTANDS YOU.

I GREW UP IN MOROCCO.

I WAS RAISED AS A MOROCCAN GIRL,
IN A CONSERVATIVE FAMILY AND
NEIGHBORHOOD. YET NOW,
IN SOCIETY, I'M SEEN AS A SLUT!
I'M A SLUT FOR DOING WHAT I LOVE
— FOR BEING MYSELF —
WHEN I'VE NEVER HARMED ANYONE IN
MY LIFE! AND I'M NOT AN ISOLATED CASE:
THERE ARE THOUSANDS OF CITIZENS LIKE ME
IN MOROCCO, JUDGED FOR WHAT THEY ARE.
BUT DON'T WORRY, WE'RE STRONGER
THAN THEY THINK,
AND WE'RE GOING TO FIGHT!

الزين مانشوفوتش؟

In my country, I'm sick of rape, harassment, patriarchy, homophobia, 'honour' killings, gender-based violence, social judgment, the control of sexuality and bodies, the imposition of ideas on others, the beating and killing of free women, non-Muslims and homosexuals, and being afraid to talk about it...

I'm sick and tired of our failing system, of these disasters being ignored by the authorities, and nobody trying to put a stop to them.

Instead of trying to solve them, they always come up with
excuses, like: 'These problems exist in every country';
'Liberating sexuality will only make the situation worse';
'There are other more important social problems'...
All I know is that all social problems are important.
All I see every day are victims who need help.

I'm fed up with the fact that
most Moroccans dream of living
in Europe or the U.S.
Why can't we live in peace
in our own land?

LiBERTÉ

When we liberate our bodies and our sexuality from the norms of society, we are accused of copying the West! The West never invented freedom and sexuality; it simply preceded us in understanding the meaning of freedom. Society is certainly not perfect there, but I believe that we are in a much more critical situation than over there. And it will take a long time for the MENA region to change mentalities and emerge from this dark period.

In conclusion, freedom and sexuality are part of human nature. They have no nationality or label. Letting others choose their sexuality is not a return to animality; rather, it's a huge step forward in ending sexual frustration and finally making peace with our bodies and our desires.

EUROPE♥

sexy

I ADMIT THAT NOT ALL MOROCCANS
ARE READY YET FOR SUCH A CHANGE.
WE NEED TO DEVELOP SEX EDUCATION FOR
YOUNG PEOPLE AND MAKE COUPLES AWARE
OF THEIR RESPONSIBILITIES. WE'LL NEED
TO TALK ABOUT CONSENT PRIOR TO THE
SEXUAL ACT, AND EXPLAIN THAT
GIVING BIRTH TO A CHILD
MEANS ENSURING ITS FUNDAMENTAL
RIGHTS AND EDUCATING IT TO CREATE A
NEW GENERATION THAT RESPECTS HUMAN
RIGHTS AND INDIVIDUAL FREEDOMS.
BUT LET'S BE CLEAR:
FREEING SEXUAL RELATIONS DOESN'T MEAN
SCREWING ANYONE AT ANY TIME!
RESPECT FOR OTHERS MUST BE LEARNED
BEFORE WE CAN LEARN TO SATISFY
OUR OWN DESIRES.

1. SEX EDUCATION

Sexual intercourse is the physical activity we engage
in to reproduce ourselves, or for simple sexual pleasure.
The latter can take the form of vaginal, oral or anal
intercourse. Sexual games include masturbation,
sexual accessories and fantasies.

All this is expressed in two dimensions,
emotional and physical, and is based on pleasure,
consent and sharing.

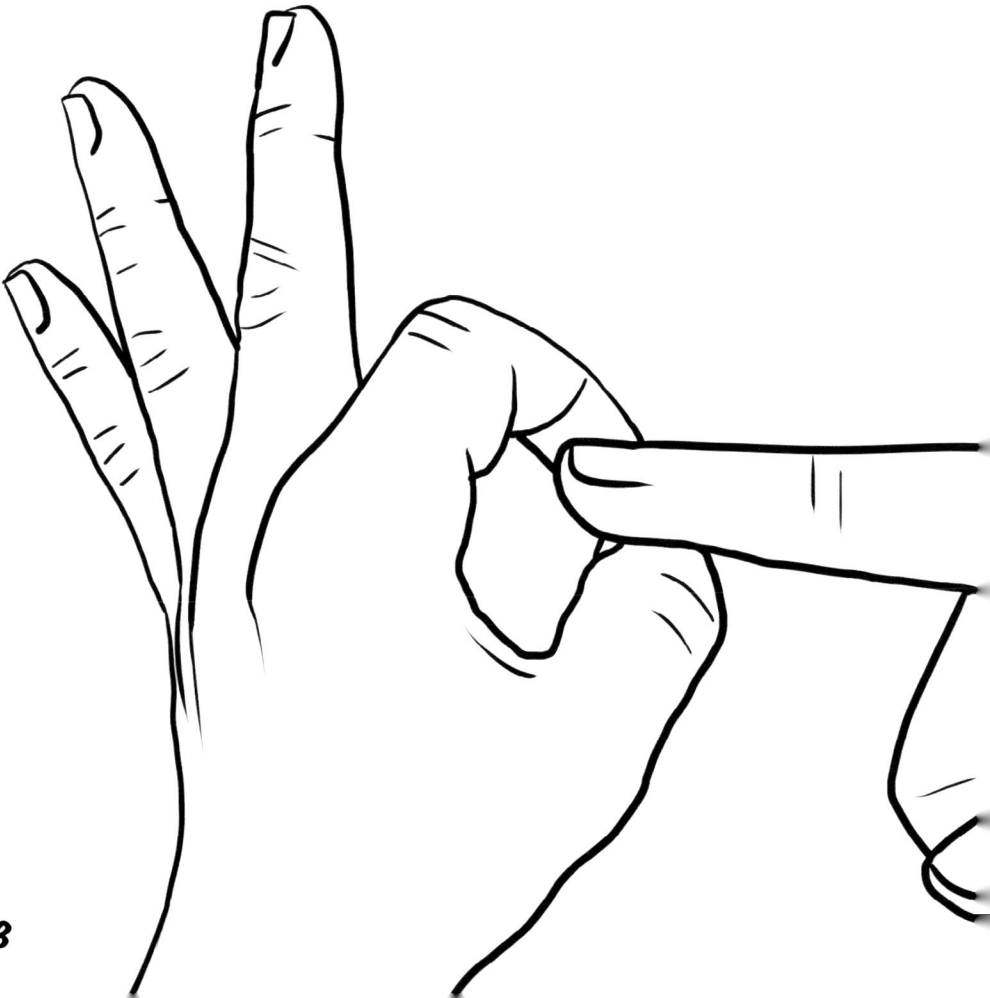

In my country, sexual relations are only legal within the framework of marriage. Heterosexuality is presented as the only possible and legal sexual orientation. It's called 'heteronormativity'. Yet the sexual act is not always between a man and a woman. It can also take place between people of the same gender, or between several people – not to mention solitary pleasure. In fact, there are almost as many sexual practices as there are individuals on earth, but none of them can do without the consent of those involved.

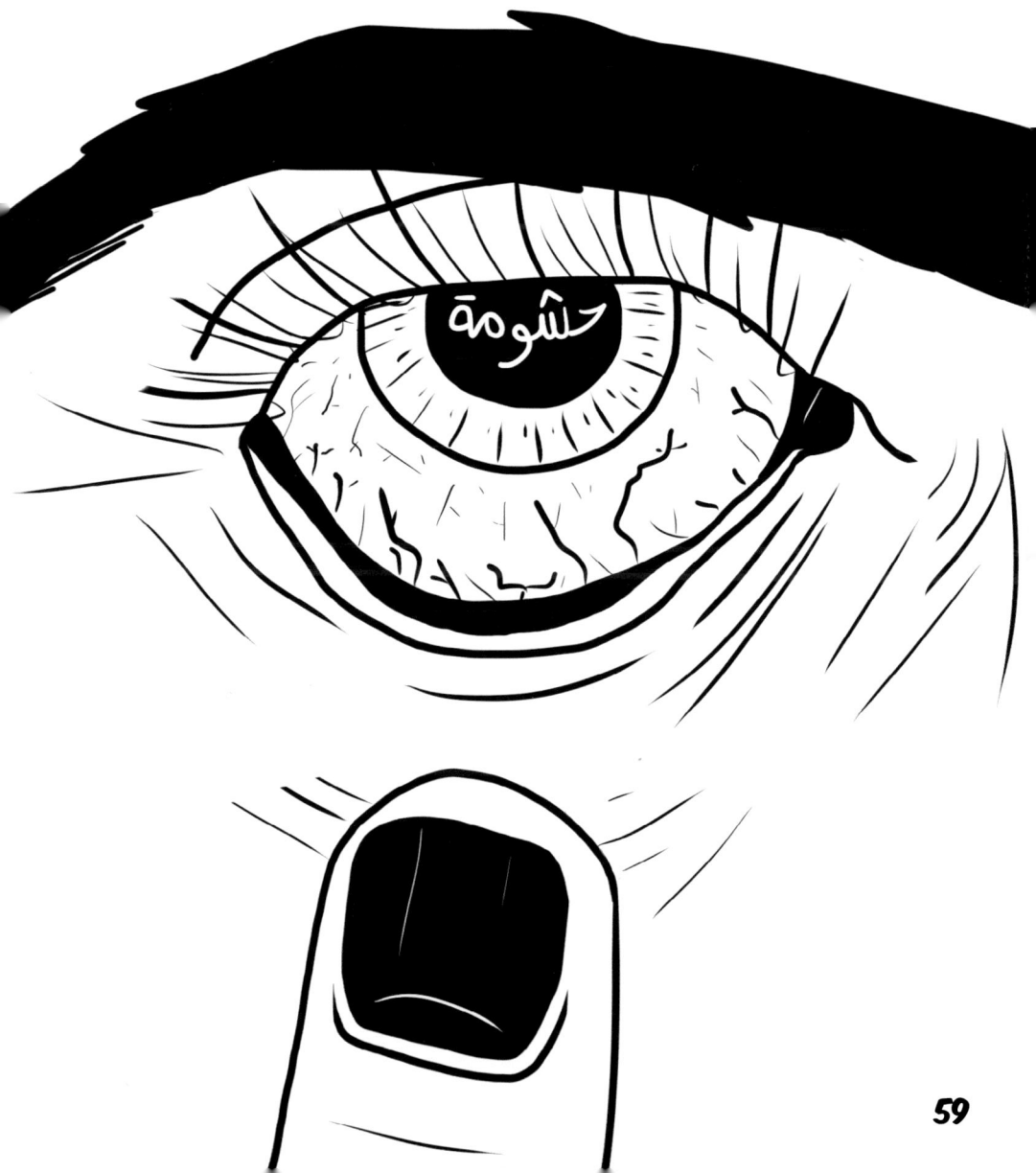

SEXUAL ORIENTATION IS THE
SEXUAL AND EMOTIONAL ATTRACTION
WE FEEL TOWARDS OTHERS,
WHETHER OF THE SAME,
OPPOSITE OR DIFFERENT GENDER.
THERE ARE MANY SEXUAL
ORIENTATIONS TODAY:
HETEROSEXUAL, HOMOSEXUAL,
BISEXUAL, ASEXUAL, AROMANTIC,
SEMIROMANTIC, DEMISEXUAL,
PANSEXUAL, POLYSEXUAL,
SAPIOSEXUAL, SKOLIOSEXUAL,
AUTOSEXUAL, ETC.

Our sexual orientation can change over the course of our lives and, above all, it's normal to be curious during adolescence. I hope that one day, in my country, sexual orientation will become an individual freedom and will no longer be imposed by society or the law. For example, even though everyone now recognizes that homosexuality is not an illness, some Moroccans still associate it with paedophilia or a crime. What makes sexual orientation acceptable is the consent of people who have reached puberty and who are no longer minors.

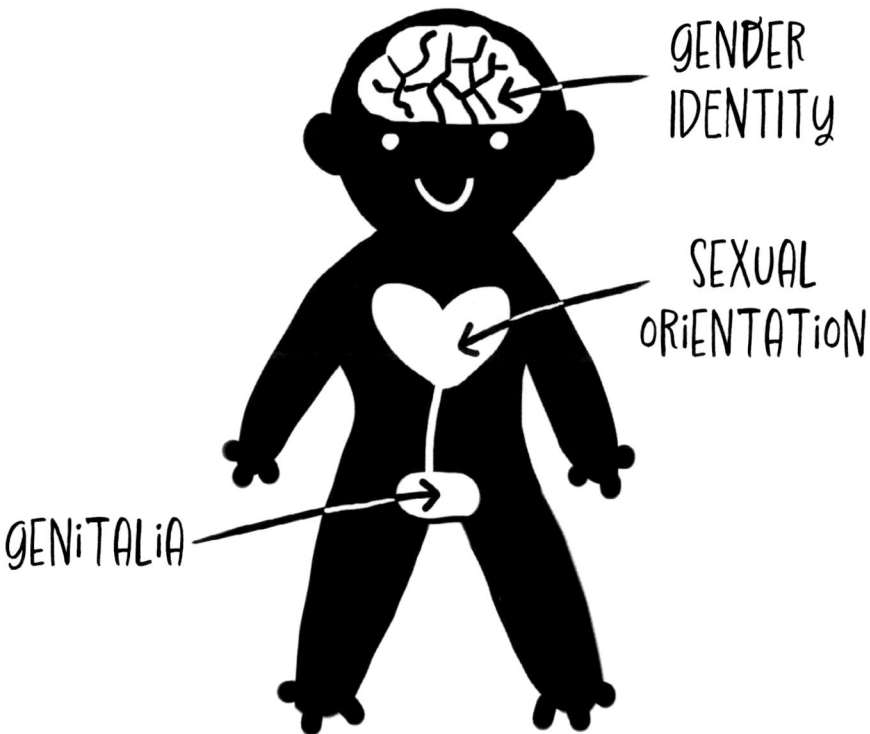

GENDER IDENTITY

SEXUAL ORIENTATION

GENITALIA

Seduction is the art with which most romantic relationships begin. Some people are afraid to take the initiative and fear rejection. So, let's make peace with this stage, and learn that, no matter what happens, life goes on!
And above all, let's seduce others with respect, otherwise it will become harassment, which is obviously a crime.

In my country, romance and love are big taboos. A kiss on television is a nightmare for families, who then immediately change the channel when faced with this scene. Blood and violence — on the screen or in the street — have become habitual, so why should a kiss or a cuddle scare us? We have to stop being afraid of kissing and hugging in public or in private. It's not a crime, and it will convince others to show love even more.

Unfortunately, we fall in love with someone under the influence of social status, economic status, beauty or even out of self-interest, for example for legal reasons or to get out of our personal situation. Borders and political regimes have managed to damage our sexual attraction, our love life and even our fantasies!

I LOVE YOU

I WANT A NEW NATIONALITY

SEXUAL INTERCOURSE CAN TAKE PLACE WITHOUT LOVE, FOR A NIGHT OR OVER A LONG PERIOD OF TIME. THIS TYPE OF SEXUALITY IS ALWAYS FROWNED UPON, EVEN THOUGH IT'S A CHOICE THAT OTHERS SHOULD RESPECT

And let's not forget the big taboo in Morocco: orgasm! It has many benefits for our physical and mental health... So, why should we be ashamed of it? We also need to stop being afraid of masturbation, because this act is just as beneficial to our health as intercourse is.

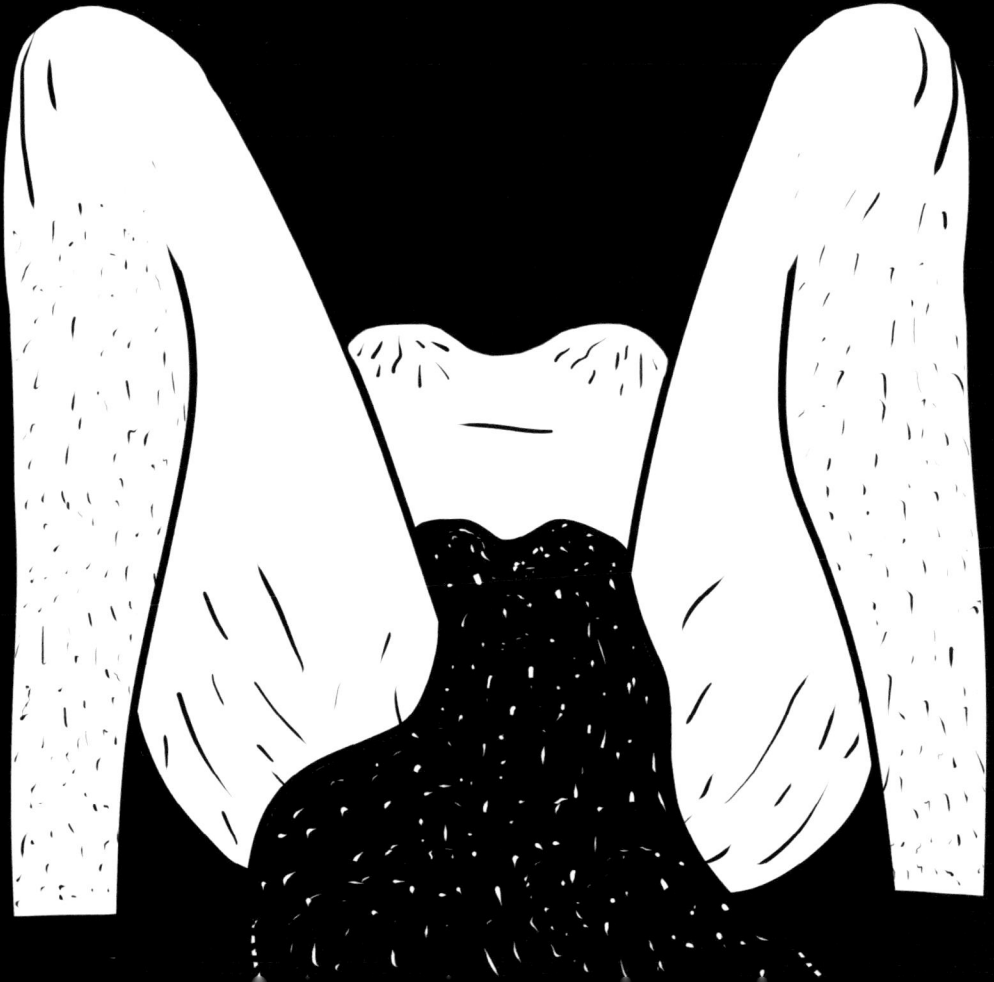

THE STAGES AND MOMENTS OF SEXUAL INTERCOURSE

DESIRE, EMOTION, LOVE, AFFECTION, LIBIDO, FANTASIES, SEDUCTION, SENSUALITY, FLIRTING, WORDS, MASTURBATION, TOUCHING, EROGENOUS ZONES, FOREPLAY, AROUSAL, KISSING, CARESSING, ERECTION, HARD-ON, PLEASURE, LUBRICATION, TONGUES, PRE-EJACULATORY FLUID, PENETRATION, SWELLING OF CLITORIS AND LABIA, SUCKING, LICKING, ORAL SEX, ANAL, POSITIONS, SEX TOYS, ORGASM, MOANING, EJACULATION.

HIV (human immunodeficiency virus) weakens the immune system and makes it vulnerable to infections, including AIDS (acquired immunodeficiency syndrome). AIDS is transmitted sexually through semen and vaginal secretions, through the blood, during childbirth and through breast milk. If left untreated, the consequences can be fatal.

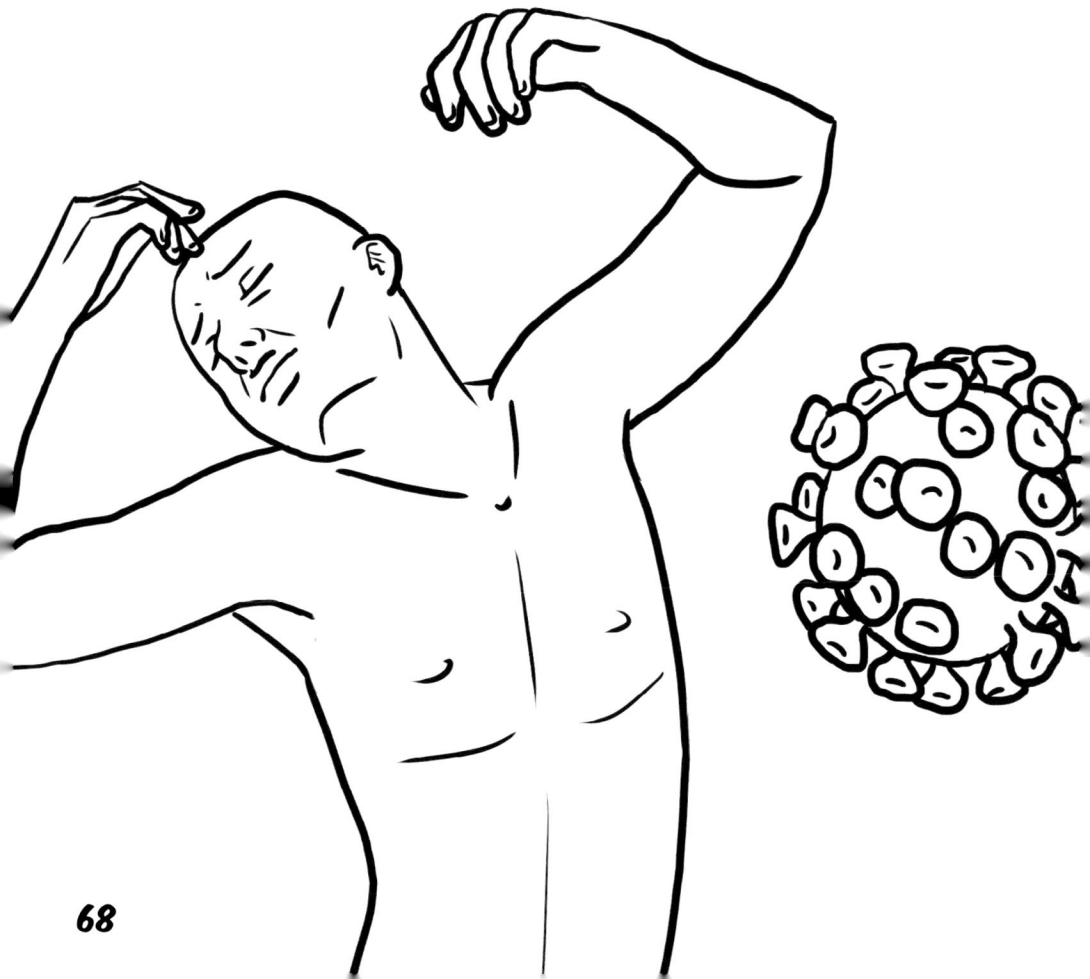

TO AVOID CONTAMINATING YOUR PARTNERS, OR TO GET TREATED IN TIME, IT'S A GOOD IDEA TO GET TESTED FOR HIV. PEOPLE WHO HAVE SEXUAL RELATIONS, WITH VAGINAL OR ANAL PENETRATION OR ORAL SEX, MUST PROTECT THEMSELVES FROM SEXUALLY-TRANSMITTED INFECTIONS BY USING CONDOMS. THIS APPLIES WHETHER THE RELATIONSHIP IS STABLE OR CASUAL.

TO AVOID UNWANTED PREGNANCY, THERE ARE SEVERAL METHODS OF CONTRACEPTION: MALE OR FEMALE CONDOMS, THE PILL FOR WOMEN AND MEN, IUDS (INTRAUTERINE DEVICES), DIAPHRAGMS, NATURAL CONTRACEPTION, TUBAL LIGATION, PERMANENT CONTRACEPTION, PATCHES, IMPLANTS, VAGINAL RINGS, CERVICAL CAPS, SPERMICIDES, STERILIZATION, INJECTABLE PROGESTINS, HORMONE INJECTIONS, HEAT-BASED CONTRACEPTION, ETC.

In Morocco, there's a big lack of awareness about contraception, which leads to huge social problems. Of course, everyone is responsible, and 'a child is not born with its own fortune', as the saying goes where I come from. But in reality, it's not the responsibility of the couple alone, but of the political, economic and social system as a whole.

For the many Moroccan women who have unwanted pregnancies, voluntary interruption of pregnancy remains a major taboo, illegal in the majority of cases. We are used to seeing videos on the internet of babies abandoned in public spaces by their mothers, just after birth. When they don't die, they grow up on the streets, in an orphanage or are sold. All this could be avoided by using contraception or having a legal abortion, and if being an unmarried mother wasn't considered a crime by society.

You also need to be careful about addiction: sexual intercourse, masturbation, compulsive relationships, cybersex, consumption of pornographic films... You shouldn't become obsessed with satisfying your sexual desire!

3. FRUSTRATION

While the sexual act should be a pleasure, a biological need and a fundamental right, in Morocco it can only legally take place within the framework of a heterosexual marriage. For me, this restriction is partly responsible for the violence (verbal and physical) that is rife in my society. It puts obstacles in the way of our life of intimacy, especially when we want to have a sexual life before marriage. For Muslims, it's haram (forbidden) to have sex outside marriage, but isn't it unfortunate to apply this rule to non-Muslims? Especially as many Muslims don't respect these prohibitions... and even admit to being against them.

عيب

Having a job and financial independence are necessary elements for a successful marriage in our country, but as these conditions are not within the reach of everyone, especially young people, they obviously can't get married. As a result, young Moroccans can't satisfy their sexual desires in a marital setting. Some end up buying privacy in hotels, cars, but also at the beach, at the cinema, in parks, cafés, toilets, during shows... and most of the time, this implies a corrupt relationship between the couple and the people in charge of such places.

Not forgetting the looks of others, judgments
of the neighbourhood, family and society.
The women concerned are then insulted, they
are accused of inciting rape and attacking
honour (while men are always encouraged
to multiply their conquests in order
to be recognized and respected).

HENCE MY QUESTION:
SHOULD THE SEXUAL ACT
OUTSIDE OF MARRIAGE
AND THE CHOICE OF SEXUAL
ORIENTATION BE DECRIMINALIZED?
SHOULD PEOPLE BE JUDGED
BY THEIR LIFE AND
SEXUAL PREFERENCES?
CAN WE ENVISAGE ALTERNATIVE
SOLUTIONS THAT MAINTAIN
THE SOCIAL ORDER
BUT RESPECT THE
FREEDOMS OF ALL
COMMUNITIES IN MOROCCO?

4. CONSENT

Unfortunately, sexual relations are not always based on consent. They can occur as a result of violent acts of various kinds.

Sexual harassment can be physical, verbal, non-verbal or moral. It is the act of repeatedly imposing comments or behaviours of a sexual nature on a person. Sexual harassment is everywhere: on public transport, at work, at school, in the street, at home, and today on the internet in the form of 'cyber harassment' (blackmail by posting intimate photos online, texting, video calls). A law in Morocco punishes harassment, but it's difficult to prove, and society always sees the victim, especially the woman, as the guilty party, whereas it's the harasser!

Rape: an act in which one person forces another to have sexual intercourse using violence.

Rape can take place even if the victim has already shown signs of tenderness (kissing, caressing). Whatever the situation, consent must be expressed. The same applies to marital relationships: marriage does not give the right to sexual relations without the consent of the spouse. Rape sometimes occurs within a family – in which case it's known as incest – and unfortunately sometimes involves under-age children (paedophilia). Many rapes also occur under the influence of drugs and alcohol.

Some rapists film and torture their victims, then blackmail them sexually or financially, or use revenge porn / 'sextortion' to publish naked photos, videos or text messages without their permission. Sometimes rape takes the form of condom removal just before ejaculation. Then there's sex trafficking, and the rape of sex workers in pornography and prostitution. The difficulties of finding work, financing one's studies and feeding one's family lead many women and men to prostitute themselves, on an occasional or permanent basis, which is also a violation of their rights.

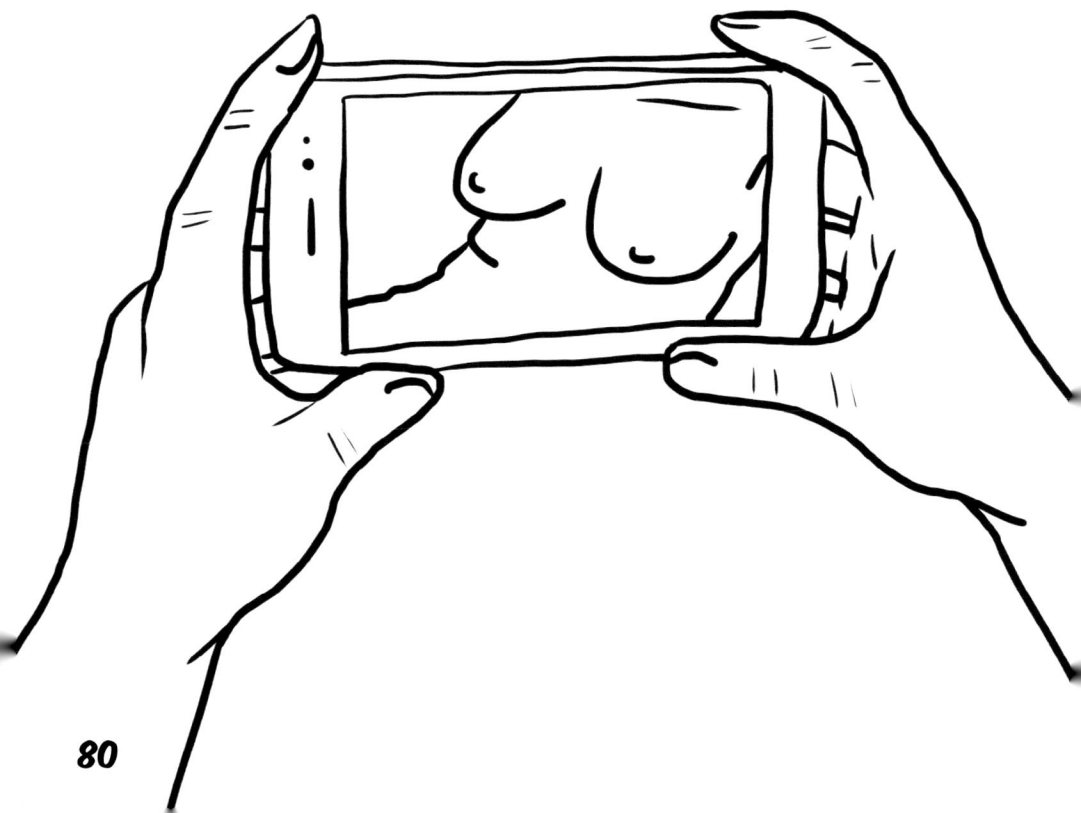

IN MY COUNTRY, IT IS VERY DIFFICULT
FOR VICTIMS TO LODGE A COMPLAINT,
BECAUSE THEY WILL BE ACCUSED
(BY THE POLICE, THE COURTS, THE FAMILY
AND SOCIETY) OF HAVING PROVOKED THEIR
ATTACKERS BY THE WAY THEY WERE DRESSED,
THE TIME OR THE PLACE WHERE THEY WERE ALONE...
THE ATTACKERS ARE RARELY CONVICTED, BECAUSE
IT IS UP TO THE VICTIMS TO PROVIDE PROOF
OF THEIR RAPE. DESPITE THE LAW, IF A VICTIM
WISHES TO SPEAK OUT, SHE MUST
BE PSYCHOLOGICALLY PREPARED TO FACE
THE JUDGMENT OF OTHERS. THIS ENCOURAGES
RAPISTS EVEN MORE, BECAUSE THEY KNOW THEY
ARE SAFE FROM PUNISHMENT. RAPE IS OBVIOUSLY
NOT ONLY COMMITTED BY MEN, BUT THE MOST
COMMON CASE IS THAT OF MEN AGAINST WOMEN.
SO, LET'S STOP BLAMING THE VICTIMS AND
START BLAMING THE RAPISTS!

AND TO DO THIS, WE NEED TO RAISE SOCIETY'S
AWARENESS, SO THAT IT NO LONGER SEES
A FREE WOMAN AS SOMEONE WHO INVITES
OTHERS TO HAVE SEX WITH HER

5. SEXUALITY: PARENTS, FAMILY

If the sexual act is *hshouma* for young people, it is even more so for their parents, especially after a long marriage with children. Sexual relations in a marriage diminish over the years, as the home is shared with other family members. Our parents live with their children, but also sometimes with their brothers and sisters, and even their own parents. Cohabitation restricts the couple's space for intimacy. Having responsibilities also reduces the libido. Stress at work, the mental burden for women who have to reconcile work and family life, financial difficulties... These torments erase the affection and tenderness of parents towards each other, but also towards their children.

IF TALKING ABOUT SEXUALITY
IS OFTEN COMPLICATED FOR
PARENTS THE WORLD OVER, IT'S
A REAL TABOO IN MOROCCO.

TOPICS RELATED TO SEXUALITY
(CONTRACEPTION, THE BODY, LOVE,
RAPE, INTIMACY, ETC.) ARE NOT
DISCUSSED WITHIN THE FAMILY.
AS A RESULT, CHILDREN LOOK FOR
INFORMATION ON THE INTERNET
AND IN THE STREET, WHICH ARE
NEITHER RELIABLE SOURCES NOR A
REFLECTION OF SEXUAL DIVERSITY.

Lack of communication between parents and children leads to conflict and misunderstanding. Parents then decide to control their offspring's movements, sometimes in different ways. By withholding pocket money, for example, they prevent teenagers from going to the movies, having coffee with their sweethearts or even traveling... In other words, they separate their youngsters from the experiences that would enable them to understand sexuality, to stop seeing it as a shame and a sin...

Parents must no longer ignore their responsibility. Raising a child also means explaining sexuality to them. 'What about school then?', you may ask. Certainly, in secondary school, sexual relations are discussed, but most students graduate this course without having any real knowledge of the subject. I remember the students in my class laughing their heads off... Even for me, it felt like a total disgrace to study it, and it was out of the question to ask my family if we didn't understand something.
So, I wish all Moroccan schoolchildren could receive sex education from a teacher or a specialist...

UNFORTUNATELY, AS YOUNG MOROCCANS LEARN NOTHING ABOUT SEXUALITY EITHER AT HOME OR AT SCHOOL... THEY LEARN BY WATCHING PORNOGRAPHIC FILMS AND DISCUSSING WITH THEIR FRIENDS. THIS IS THE SOURCE OF ALL OUR SOCIAL DISASTERS. AND MOST MOROCCAN PARENTS SEE THEIR CHILDREN AS COPIES OF THEMSELVES: THEIR OFFSPRING MUST BELIEVE IN THEIR IDEAS, HAVE THE SAME JOB AND MARRY SOMEONE THEY LIKE. IF YOU GIVE BIRTH TO A CHILD, BE READY TO ACCEPT IT AS IT IS. OTHERWISE, REST ASSURED: YOU'RE GIVING BIRTH TO A CHILD WHO'S GOING TO STRUGGLE.

6. SEXUALITY IN OR OUTSIDE MARRIAGE

OUTSIDE MARRIAGE

In my country, any sexual act outside marriage is strictly forbidden by law. Yet many Moroccans disobey the law, and even live together without being married. They hide their sex lives from public authorities, society and even their families. If they are discovered, they will have to face moral judgments, prison and sometimes even enforced marriage. Many people in Morocco hide their sexuality, even though love is not a crime.

I CAN ALREADY HEAR SOME PEOPLE REPLYING: 'WHAT YOU'RE SAYING IS MADNESS'. SO I REPEAT: I'M SPEAKING ON BEHALF OF NON-MUSLIM MOROCCANS, OR SIMPLY THOSE WHO WISH TO LIVE AS THEY SEE FIT. MUSLIM MOROCCANS MUST LEARN TO KEEP THEIR RELIGIOUS DISCOURSE TO THEMSELVES. FOR THE REAL FOLLY LIES IN IMPOSING ONE'S IDEOLOGY ON OTHERS.

The relationship to sexuality is not seen in the same way by men and women. We women are constantly controlled. We have to keep our virginity until marriage, under the pretext of remaining pure, and we shouldn't discover the pleasure of masturbation because we risk breaking our hymen. As a result, we find alternative ways of living out our sexuality, such as resorting to practices that do not involve vaginal penetration, like sodomy.
We are forbidden from certain sporting activities such as cycling, gymnastics and horse-riding, supposedly to ensure that we remain virgins until we are married.

Worse still, we're sometimes forced to undergo
hymenoplasty – hymen reconstruction – or a virginity
test. This test may be required before our marriage,
but also to get a job! And, if it's negative, our lives are
in danger. In the MENA region (and still today), parents
abandon or even kill their non-virgin daughters, simply
to save the family's honour and reputation.

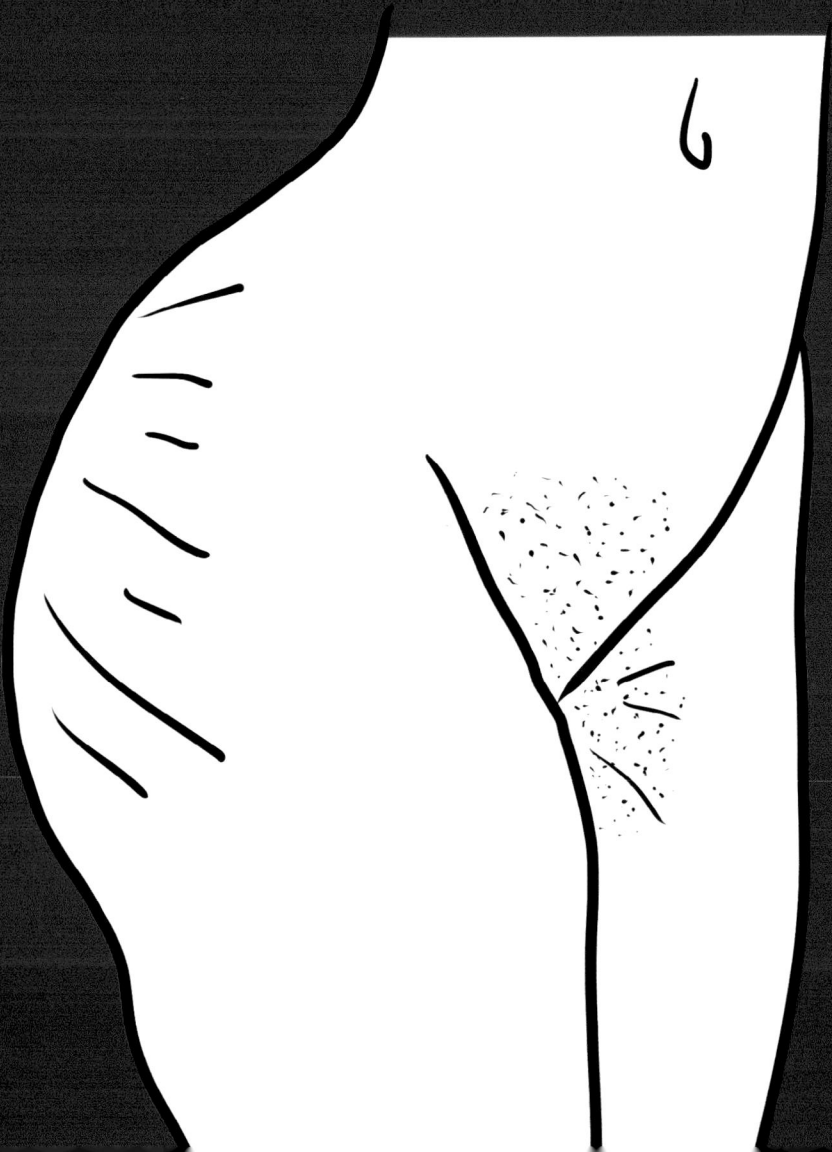

Men, on the other hand, need not worry about losing their virginity; on the contrary, they are encouraged to multiply their female conquests. Some of them even turn to prostitutes (out of curiosity, frustration or simply seeking pleasure), and live their sexuality without limits. But on their wedding day... they prefer a virgin. In general, men in my country are not judged for their sex lives.

VIRGINITY IS THEREFORE MISUNDERSTOOD BY MOST MOROCCANS. HERE ARE A FEW EXPLANATIONS. THE HYMEN IS A THIN MUCOUS MEMBRANE THAT PARTIALLY CLOSES THE ENTRANCE TO THE VAGINA, ALLOWING MENSTRUAL BLOOD TO PASS THROUGH. THE SIZE OF THIS ORIFICE IS DIFFERENT FOR EACH OF US.

WE MAY NOT BLEED DURING OUR FIRST INTERCOURSE, DEPENDING ON THE SHAPE OF OUR HYMEN; WE MAY EVEN BE BORN WITHOUT A HYMEN, OR THE HYMEN MAY NOT TEAR DURING THE FIRST PENETRATION BUT DURING SUBSEQUENT ONES, AS IT DILATES. IN FACT, IF THE FIRST PENETRATION IS AGRESSIVE, THE HYMEN TEARS AND WE BLEED, BUT IF IT'S GENTLE, THE LOSS OF VIRGINITY IS NOT NECESSARILY ACCOMPANIED BY BLEEDING.

Because the hymen is misunderstood,
because ignorance and patriarchy reign,
women have been accused and threatened with
death for an act they didn't commit. As I've explained:
virginity has nothing to do with the hymen, and
being a virgin doesn't mean being pure. We all remain
pure, even after repeated intercourse.

IN MY COUNTRY,
A MAN WANTS TO MARRY
A 'PURE' WOMAN,
EVEN IF HE'S HAD SEVERAL
SEXUAL ENCOUNTERS.
WHY IS THIS?
DO THEY MARRY
A WOMAN OR A VAGINA?

Banning sex before marriage is unfair
(because not all Moroccans are Muslims),
pointless (because it's not respected),
and dangerous (because it even leads
to rape and harassment). On the contrary,
letting others live as they like, as long
as there's consent between them,
doesn't hurt anyone.

Being single and having sex in Morocco can be expensive. In the literal sense, financially: looking for *bertoucha*, i.e. secret places to have sex. And in the physical sense, as you're subject to stress and the fear of going to prison... I suggest we focus on sexual crimes (rape, harassment, street assaults) because love and consensual sex are not crimes!

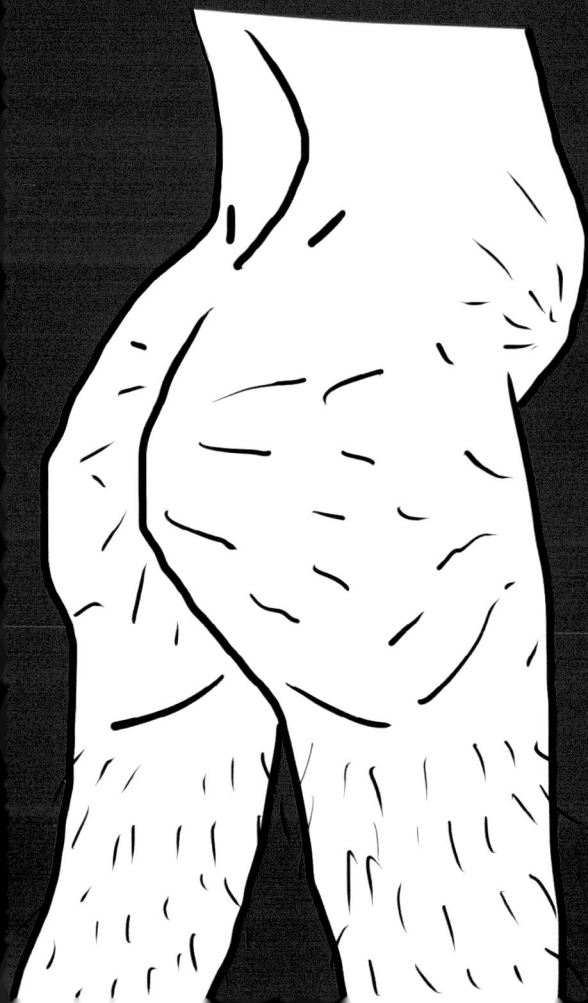

MARRIAGE

For those who have chosen to remain virgins until marriage, the wedding night will be a time of discovery. In Morocco, some people still follow the tradition of waiting until the couple have made love before going out, in front of the whole neighbourhood, to music, with their wedding dress draped in the virgin's blood. Here again, the aim is to prove to everyone the purity of the bride. But there are also modern couples who marry without being virgins, although they remain a minority.

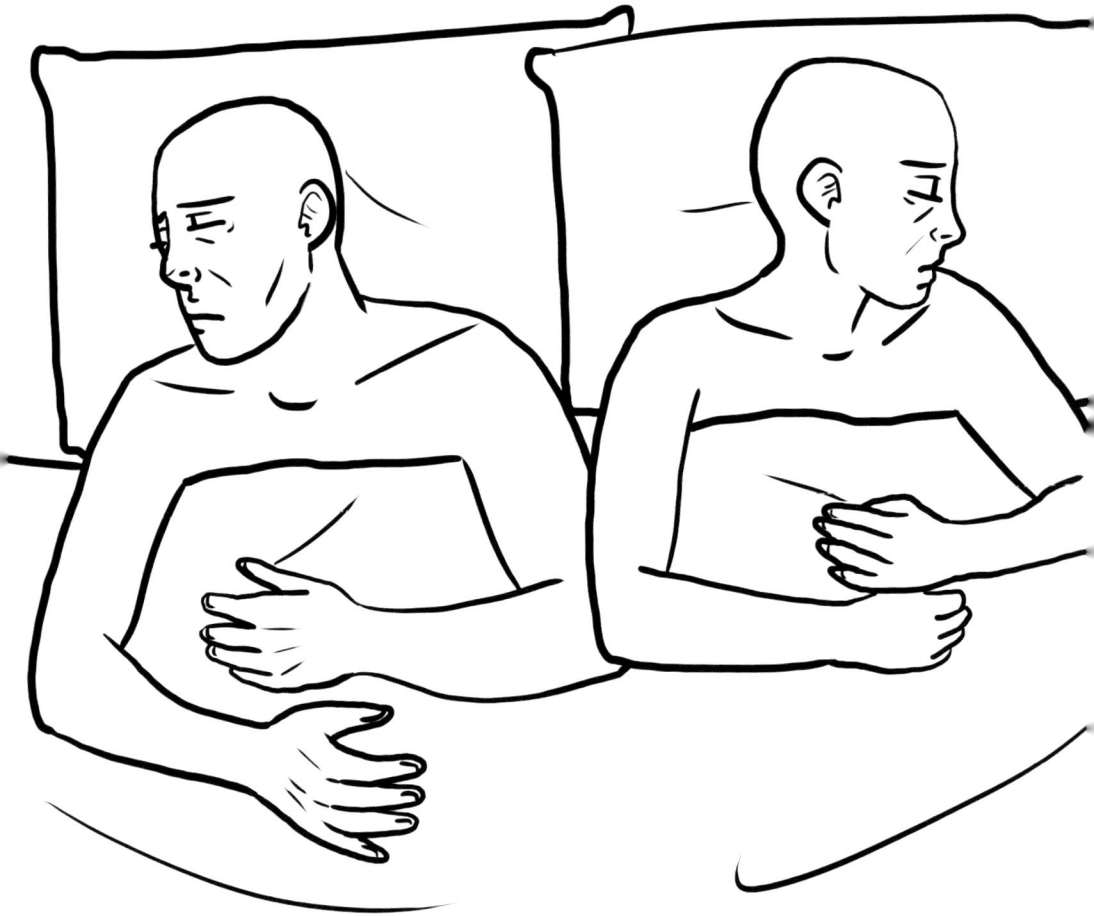

Marriage certainly has its positive aspects, such as
finally experiencing physical and spiritual love. But there
can also be disappointments: repulsion towards the
other's body, violent penetration (sodomy, beating, etc.),
premature ejaculation, frigidity, simulated orgasm.
The mismatch between spouses' expectations can
lead to sexual dissatisfaction, conflict and
tension within the couple.

This incompatibility of desire sometimes leads to adultery. Pleasure is sought outside the marital context with other people, notably prostitutes. It can also lead to the imposition of non-consensual relations – marital rape. Or it can lead to divorce, which is frowned upon by society: it's synonymous with failure, and the fault is usually attributed to the woman. Men, on the other hand, are not judged.

THIS UNFORTUNATE CHAIN OF EVENTS
BEGS THE QUESTION: WOULD EXPERIMENTING
WITH A SEX LIFE BEFORE MARRIAGE BE
USEFUL TO THE COUPLE TO TEST THEIR
COMPATIBILITY? WOULD IT HELP TO
AVOID A SAD MARRIED LIFE?

OF COURSE, YOU KNOW MY ANSWER:
YES, IT'S USEFUL! IT'S OBVIOUSLY *HARAM*,
ILLEGAL, FOR MUSLIM MOROCCANS,
BUT I REPEAT THAT I HAVE NO INTENTION
OF CHANGING ANY RELIGIOUS DISCOURSE
AND THAT I RESPECT ALL RELIGIONS.
I'M THINKING OF THE NON-MUSLIM
COMMUNITY, OBLIGED TO FOLLOW RULES
IN SPITE OF THEMSELVES, EVEN THOUGH
THEY NO LONGER CONSTITUTE A MINORITY
(WE'LL NEVER KNOW THEIR NUMBERS, AS
THEY'RE AFRAID TO DECLARE THEMSELVES).

But it gets worse.

In Morocco, marriages can be performed illegally by simply reading the first surah or verse of the Koran ('Al-Fatiha'), without signing a contract. This happens particularly to underage girls. This non-contractual alliance gives them no legal or economic protection, and if they become pregnant, they have no assurance of their rights.

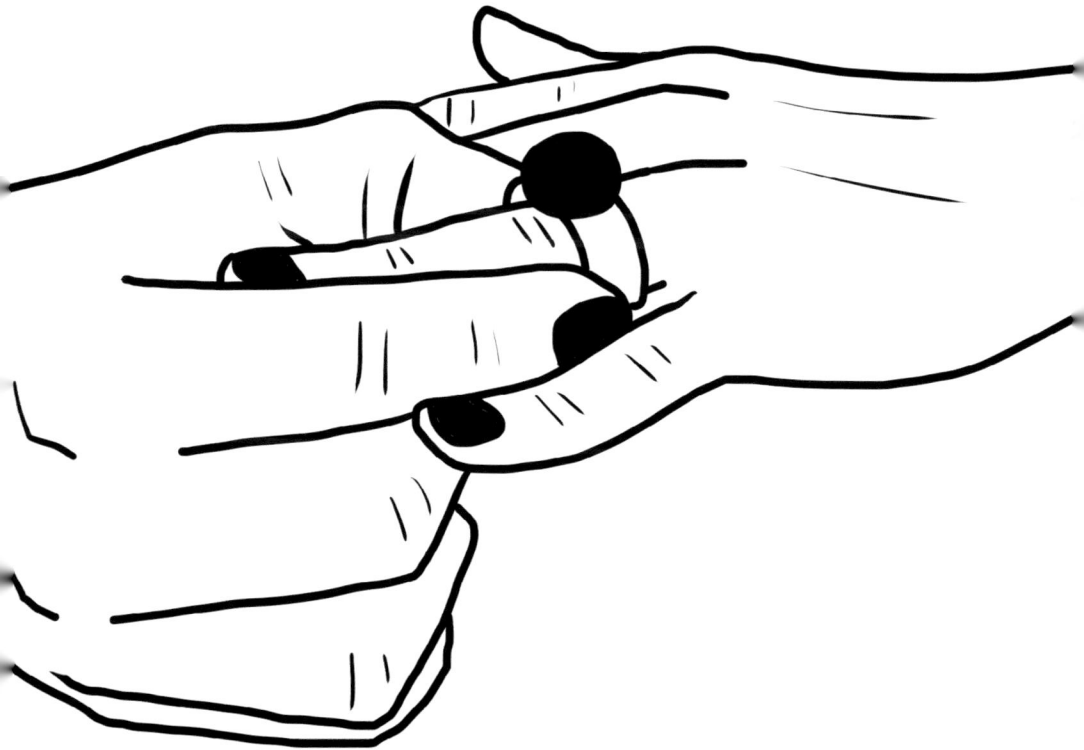

MARRIAGE IS A
RESPONSIBILITY, AND
SIGNING SUCH A CONTRACT
JUST BECAUSE YOU WANT
TO HAVE SEX AND ARE TIRED
OF WAITING, CAN GIVE RISE
TO A FAMILY THAT IS NOT
FOUNDED ON LOVE,
BUT ON FRUSTRATED
DESIRE. I LEAVE YOU TO
IMAGINE WHAT THIS TYPE OF
UNION WOULD LEAD TO OVER
THE YEARS, ESPECIALLY
WITH CHILDREN.

CONCLUSION

I'm happy to have had the chance to write about what I've experienced and observed in my beloved Moroccan society. It's because I love my country and my culture that I'm ready to do all I can to denounce the taboos that victimize people every day, and to express what most Moroccans can't.

I'M A MOROCCAN WOMAN WHO GREW UP IN A CONSERVATIVE, MIDDLE-CLASS ENVIRONMENT. I STRUGGLED AS A TEENAGER, AN ADULT, AN ARTIST, AND EVEN AS A MECHANICAL ENGINEER...

I HAD TO ADAPT TO MY SOCIETY, MY FAMILY AND MY SEXUALITY. I REALIZED THAT IT'S A CURSE TO BE BORN DIFFERENT, THAT MY LIFE WILL BE A STRUGGLE FOR EXISTENCE.

PEACE AND ART ARE THE ONLY TOOLS I USE TO INVITE MY DEAR MOROCCANS TO ACCEPT OUR DIFFERENCES.

I'M NOT TRYING TO CHANGE ANY RELIGION OR BELIEF, BUT I DO DREAM OF MUTUAL RESPECT BETWEEN ALL COMMUNITIES, SO THAT WE CAN ALL LIVE TOGETHER ON OUR LAND. MOROCCO IS A COUNTRY THAT HAS BROUGHT TOGETHER A MULTITUDE OF CULTURES AND RELIGIONS THROUGHOUT ITS HISTORY.

IT WILL ALWAYS BE MY FAVORITE COUNTRY, I'LL ALWAYS PUT HENNA ON MY HANDS AND FEET, I'LL WEAR MY CAFTANS WHILE LISTENING TO GNAWA MUSIC, I'LL NEVER FORGET THE MOROCCAN BEACHES, MOUNTAINS AND DESERTS. BUT AFTER BEING SO OFTEN BLAMED BY SOCIETY, FOR THE SOLE REASON THAT I'M A WOMAN, I FEEL THE URGENT NEED TO SPEAK OUT. BECAUSE I KNOW I'M NOT THE ONLY ONE CONCERNED.

The taboos I've tried to break here persist in different ways, depending on the region and the social nature of the community. But they're all just there to hold us back. If an act is based on consent, respect and love, we shouldn't be afraid to talk about it!

I DON'T EXPECT THIS BOOK TO
CHANGE MY SOCIETY, BUT I DO HOPE
THAT EVERY SENTENCE YOU READ HAS
PUT YOU IN THE SHOES OF ALL THE VICTIMS
OF PATRIARCHY, EXTREMISM
AND IGNORANCE.

I CALL FOR PEACE IN ALL MOROCCAN
COMMUNITIES. IF YOU MEET SOMEONE
DIFFERENT, LEARN TO
ACCEPT THEM WITH LOVE.

WE'RE ALL EQUAL HUMAN BEINGS,
AND WHILE IT'S IMPOSSIBLE TO BE ALL
THE SAME, WE CAN ALL LIVE IN PEACE.

LOVE AND PEACE,
ZAINAB FASIKI

Thanks

I would like to thank my family and my friend François F. who helped me write and publish the original edition of this book.

A huge thanks to the team of Massot Editions (for the French edition), especially you, Florent, for your confidence in me.

Thanks to all the people I've met in my events and on social networks for their support!

CONTENTS

Clairview Books Ltd.,
Russet, Sandy Lane,
West Hoathly,
W. Sussex RH19 4QQ

www.clairviewbooks.com

Published by Clairview Books 2024

Originally published in French by Massot Éditions, Paris, in 2019

© Zainab Fasiki 2019
This translation © Clairview Books 2024

A CIP catalogue record for this book is available from the British
Library

ISBN 978 1 912992 56 0

Typeset by yellowfish.design
Printed and bound by Gutenberg Press, Malta